WEEKENDS FOR TWO IN THE **SOUTHWEST**

BY BILL GLEESON | PHOTOGRAPHS BY CARY HAZLEGROVE

weekends for two

IN THE SOUTHWEST

SECOND EDITION • COMPLETELY REVISED AND UPDATED

50 ROMANTIC GETAWAYS

CHRONICLE BOOKS
SAN FRANCISCO

ACKNOWLEDGMENTS

The author wishes to thank Yvonne Gleeson
for research assistance and project coordination.
The photographer wishes to thank Sarah Hazlegrove
and Virginia Bullington.

Library of Congress Cataloging-in-Publication
Data available.

ISBN 0-8118-4624-5

Manufactured in China.

Designed and typeset by Deborah Bowman

Cover photograph: La Posada de Taos,
Taos, New Mexico

Distributed in Canada by Raincoast Books
9050 Shaughnessy Street
Vancouver, British Columbia V6P 6E5

10 9 8 7 6 5 4 3 2 1

Chronicle Books LLC
85 Second Street
San Francisco, California 94105

www.chroniclebooks.com

Table of Contents

Introduction

Before you buy a car, you take a test drive. Before you select a tomato, you give it a squeeze. Before you purchase a new outfit, you try it on. But how do you go about choosing a romantic getaway destination?

If you were Goldilocks, you could make a bed-to-bed comparison. But if you live in New York— or Phoenix, for that matter—and you're planning a trip to Sedona, dropping by for a preview probably isn't in the cards. Instead, you're more apt to take a recommendation from well-intended but not necessarily romantically enlightened friends. You might base your decision on a Web-site photo, or use a thick auto-club guide with a three-line description but no pictures.

It's a process that's about as predictable as throwing dice. Sometimes you win, sometimes you lose.

Picking a winning destination brings relaxation and coziness, which helps set the stage for romance. On the other hand, making the wrong choice can be as romantically rewarding as taking a long, cold shower alone.

In choosing fifty romantic places for our revised and updated Southwest edition, we have provided our readers with a range of accommodations in terms of rates, size, location, ambience, and setting. Our selections vary from small, inexpensive bed-and-breakfast inns to pricey, full-service luxury resorts. Settings range from remote desert oases and small villages to thriving city centers and high-mountain hideaways.

ROOMS FOR ROMANCE

When evaluating the romantic appeal of inns, hotels, and resorts for the *Weekends for Two* series, we consider the following criteria, honed through visits to hundreds of destinations. In the Southwest, our romantic checklist included:

- Private bathrooms (a must in our opinion; we'll tell you if any are shared or remote)
- In-room fireplaces
- Tubs and showers designed for two
- Breakfast in bed or in your room
- Feather beds, cushy comforters, and upscale linens
- Romantically draped beds
- Couches, love seats, *bancos,* or nooks for sitting together
- Private decks, patios, or balconies with inspirational views
- Enchanting Southwestern décor and special touches such as fresh flowers and music
- Rooms where smoking is not permitted.

Few destinations featured in this book offer a complete menu of such niceties, but each offers at least some.

We also sought out places that exude an overall, sometimes-difficult-to-describe, intimate atmosphere that engenders romance, as well as those providing pleasant service and respect for privacy.

Finally, we avoided destinations referred to in the lodging industry as "homestays." These are private homes in which a room or rooms are rented out to travelers, often by owners lacking skill in the art of innkeeping.

During our visits to each destination, we discovered special rooms that are particularly conducive to a romantic experience, and we've devoted a good part of this book to details of particularly romantic rooms and suites. When booking your getaway reservation, don't hesitate to ask about the availability of a specific room—especially if you already have a personal favorite.

TABLES FOR TWO

At the beginning of each section, we've identified particularly noteworthy restaurants near our featured destinations. These were sampled by us and/or recommended by innkeepers whose opinions we respect. Keep in mind, however, that restaurants—and chefs—come and go. Accordingly, we suggest you balance these recommendations with updates and new choices offered by your innkeeper. He or she will be happy to offer suggestions.

A WORD ABOUT RATES

Travelers scouting Southwest highways for discount lodgings can still find a no-frills motel room for under $100, but this guide isn't for bargain hunters. Though we were pleasantly surprised by the number of very reasonably priced lodgings discovered during our travels, many of the special rooms we describe are more than $200 per night, especially in popular getaway destinations like Santa Fe and Sedona.

To help you plan your getaway budget, the approximate 2006 rates for specific rooms are noted within each description. Keep in mind that an increasing number of establishments require two-night minimum stays on weekends and holidays, so plan your budget accordingly.

In the Southwest, rates frequently vary with seasons, with high season (or "in season") commanding the steepest tariffs. Keep in mind, however, that the high season varies from climate to climate and inn to inn. In hotter locales like Tucson, high season could be October through April, while in temperate Sedona, the high season usually runs from March through mid-November. In Santa Fe and Taos, whose comparatively cool summers attract travelers from the simmering lowlands, high season generally runs from May through October. Bargains are often available during low season (or "off season").

High-season rates per couple are classified at the end of each listing in the following ranges, not including tax:

Moderate: Under $200

Expensive: $200 – $300

Deluxe: Over $300

FINAL NOTES

No payment was sought or accepted from any establishment in exchange for being featured in this book. We make the decisions about which properties to include and how they're described.

Food, wine, and flowers were occasionally added to our photo scenes for styling purposes. Some inns provide these amenities; others do not. Please ask when making a reservation whether these items are complimentary or whether they're provided for an extra charge.

Also, please understand that we cannot guarantee that these properties will maintain furnishings or standards as they existed at the time of our visit. We very much appreciate hearing from readers if their experience is at variance with our descriptions. Reader comments are carefully consulted in the creation and revision of each *Weekends for Two* volume. You may reach us at www.billgleeson.com. Your opinions are critical.

DAYTIME DIVERSIONS

Valley of the Sun shoppers head for The Borgata, Biltmore
Fashion Park, and Scottsdale Fashion Square shopping
centers, among many others. Tower Plaza Mall holds one
of two ice-skating rinks in PHOENIX (the other is Ozzie
Ice), and there's a huge IMAX theater in TEMPE.

 The Phoenix Zoo, open daily, is home to more than
one thousand critters, while the Desert Botanical Garden
in Papago Park boasts more than ten thousand cacti.
Ask your innkeeper about Phoenix-area horseback rides.

 On the outskirts of TUCSON, Saguaro National
Monument is home to hundreds of thousands of the multi-
armed sentinels, which are native only to the Sonoran
Desert. A tram system transports day-trippers into Sabino
Canyon, famous for its waterfalls and natural pools.

 There are extensive collections of pre-Columbian and
Western art at the Tucson Museum of Art. Also in Tucson,
the Arizona-Sonora Desert Museum is considered one
of the world's finest showcases of natural wonders.

 Visitors to mile-high BISBEE will want to browse
the town's antiques shops, art galleries, and gift shops.
You can even explore an inactive copper mine. Excursions
from Bisbee include Tombstone, Cochise Stronghold, and
Ramsey Canyon Preserve.

TABLES FOR TWO

Café Roka, BISBEE
Cowboy Ciao, 7133 East Stetson Drive, SCOTTSDALE
Christopher's, 2584 East Camelback Road, PHOENIX
Bavarian Point, 4815 East Main Street, MESA
The American Grill, 1233 South Alma School Road, MESA
Janos, 3770 East Sunrise Drive, TUCSON
The Vivace, 4310 North Campbell Avenue, TUCSON
Café Poca Cosa, 88 East Broadway, TUCSON

SOUTHERN ARIZONA

THE FACTS
Fifteen rooms, seven with private baths and parlors.
Complimentary full breakfast served at tables for two.
Old West–style saloon. No disabled access. Moderate.

GETTING THERE
From Interstate 10, drive south on Highway 80 through
Tombstone to Bisbee. Hotel is on Main Street, downtown.

BISBEE GRAND HOTEL
57 Main Street
Bisbee, AZ 85603
Telephone: (520) 432-5900;
toll-free: (800) 421-1909
www.bisbeegrandhotel.com

Picture a Western movie in which a lady in red and a grizzled cowboy kick up their heels in a smoky saloon and later disappear together up a darkened stairway, and you'll have a fairly accurate impression of the legendary Bisbee Grand Hotel in its heyday. Today's visitors to this storied hostelry are doubtlessly more refined than the rough-and-tumble folk who inhabited these parts a century ago, but there's still plenty here to remind the two of you of old Arizona.

Guests get their first taste of old Bisbee when checking in at a restored century-old saloon on the hotel's ground floor. Some of the fixtures here were once owned by legendary Tombstone lawman Wyatt Earp. The antique back bar actually came from Tombstone's Pony Saloon.

ROOMS FOR ROMANCE

One of the most unusual guest rooms you'll ever experience is the Old Western Suite (mid $100 range), where guests bunk in a queen-sized bed positioned inside an authentically styled covered wagon. This unique suite also features a spa tub for two and shares a sitting room with the adjacent Hollywood Western Suite, a newer accommodation that features the visages of Western movie legends John Wayne, Hopalong Cassidy, Gene Autry, and Tom Mix. Guests are also treated to a spa tub for two as well as a separate shower.

The aptly named Victorian Suite (mid $100 range) is one of two sensuous front-facing suites. Sporting a blushingly bawdy décor, the suite is decorated with a canopy bed draped in flowing red fabric. French doors separate the bedroom from a sitting room containing a tiny antique love seat and a tiled decorative fireplace.

Next door is the Oriental Suite (mid $100 range), a lovers' lair appointed with an ornate king-sized antique Chinese teak wedding bed. Described by the hotel's proprietor as an "adult play pen," it's one of the most appealing beds we found in our Southwest travels. The suite's sitting room has a couch and a decorative fireplace.

After we visited, the hotel announced the opening of a set of annex suites including the Sky Suite (mid $100 range) and the Old Bisbee Suite (low $100 range), both of which are part of the Cliff House just up the street.

THE FACTS

Five rooms, each with private bath. Complimentary full gourmet breakfast served at a communal table and tables for two, in your room, or outdoors, weather permitting. No disabled access. Two-night minimum stay required during holiday periods. Moderate.

GETTING THERE

From Interstate 10 in Tucson, take Speedway exit and drive east to Euclid Avenue. Turn right and follow to University Boulevard. Turn right; inn is on left.

THE PEPPERTREES INN

There's something about a college town that stirs our romantic souls. Maybe it's that the ever-present examples of young love remind us of our own youthful college days of passions and dreams.

We rediscovered that energizing spirit on the campus of the University of Arizona, and followed it down the street to the Peppertrees. You don't have to be a student to savor this delightful inn, which shares a downtown neighborhood with sorority and fraternity houses.

The quaint turn-of-the-century home that serves as the centerpiece of this compound took its name from the California pepper trees that once presided over the property.

On the pretty, flower-filled rear courtyard, many college romances blossom each year into wedding ceremonies. Guests have easy access to the university campus and to Tucson's Fourth Avenue shopping district, either by foot (it's just minutes away) or by a renovated trolley, which rolls along University Boulevard in front of the inn.

ROOMS FOR ROMANCE

Our favorites are the two rooms in the guest house at the rear of the property. Sunset (around $200) has a living room with a television and a couch, a full kitchen, and a small private patio reached by French doors. Upstairs are two bedrooms, one with a queen-sized bed, and a small bathroom with a tub-and-shower combination. The adjacent Sunrise suite has a similar floor plan.

In the annex, Phoebe's Room (low $100 range) has a king-sized bed, 1930s furnishings, and a private bathroom with a shower stall. It shares a living room with the front-facing Jenny's Room.

In the main house, Penelope's Room (low $100 range) is a lovely room with five windows and a cushioned church pew, but the private bathroom is located across the hall.

THE PEPPERTREES INN
724 East University Boulevard
Tucson, AZ 85719
Telephone: (520) 622-7167;
toll-free: (800) 348-5763
www.peppertreesinn.com

15

THE FACTS

Fifty 1- and 2-bedroom suites, each with private bath, kitchen, and oversized tub. Restaurants, lounge, two 18-hole golf courses, a driving range, twelve tennis courts, a swimming pool, and exercise rooms. Disabled access. Smoking allowed. No minimum stay requirement. Deluxe.

GETTING THERE

From Interstate 10 in Tucson, exit at Ina Road and drive east to Skyline. Turn right on Skyline (which becomes Sunrise), and follow to Kolb Road. Turn left on Kolb and drive a half-mile to Ventana Canyon Golf and Racquet Club gatehouse on right.

THE LODGE AT VENTANA CANYON
6200 North Clubhouse Lane
Tucson, AZ 85750
Telephone: (520) 577-4010;
toll-free: (800) 828-5701
www.thelodgeatventanacanyon.com

THE LODGE AT VENTANA CANYON

Would you prefer experiencing the magnificent Sonoran Desert from a couch in your private air-conditioned living room, from a refreshing pool, from a hiking path, or from a lush fairway lined with saguaro cacti? If your answer is "all of the above," you'll likely enjoy this resort as much as we did.

Our personal favorite Southwest desert destination, The Lodge at Ventana Canyon is the quintessence of the all-in-one luxury resort, providing a generous range of activities, from recreation to romance.

Overlooking Tucson from the foothills of the Santa Catalina Mountains, the resort entices travelers with not one, but two 18-hole PGA golf courses, a huge swimming pool, and a dozen lighted tennis courts. There are also fully equipped exercise rooms and two restaurants.

ROOMS FOR ROMANCE

The resort's fifty 1- and 2-bedroom suites each has a kitchen, a separate living room with cushy furnishings, multiple televisions and telephones, a spacious and well-equipped bathroom with an oversized tub, and a private balcony or patio with views of the Santa Catalina Mountains or the city of Tucson. Keep in mind that the rates noted below drop substantially during the summer months; high season is usually mid-January through mid-April.

Suite 229 (around $400) is the one most often requested by honeymooners and romantics in-the-know. Boasting approximately nine hundred square feet, it has a king-sized bed and overlooks a fairway and the distant mountains.

One way to soften the high-season tariff would be to visit with another couple and share the cost of a two-bedroom suite (around $600). For example, suite 221, our apartment-sized two-bedroom unit, was equipped with a kitchenette, a spacious living room, a master bedroom, a loft bedroom reached by a circular stairway, and two well-equipped bathrooms. One of these held a deep soaking-tub-and-shower combination.

THE FACTS

Eighty-six rooms and suites, each with private bath; thirteen with fireplaces. Heated swimming pool, clay tennis courts, two restaurants, and lounge. Disabled access. Smoking allowed. No minimum stay requirement. Moderate to deluxe.

GETTING THERE

From Interstate 10 in Tucson, exit on Speedway Boulevard and drive east on Speedway to Campbell Avenue. Turn left and drive a half mile to Elm Street. Turn right and follow a half mile to inn on right.

As the story goes, Isabella Greenway, who built the Arizona Inn in the early 1930s, was a stickler for detail. Some still remember her wandering the construction site with a pillow, assuming recumbent positions to make firsthand judgments about where to place a window for just the right view from bed.

That fine-tuned attention to comfort is still embraced by Isabella's family members, who have carefully preserved and nurtured this fabled grande dame of southern Arizona resorts for more than half a century.

A lush retreat in the midst of busy Tucson, Arizona Inn occupies fourteen colorful acres of mature trees, gardens, and lawns. Its clientele ranges from families to businesspeople, not to mention the many couples who find this timeless resort an inspiring year-round romantic-getaway destination.

The inn has a reputation as a retreat for well-heeled travelers, and well-to-do locals as well as celebrities are drawn to its highly rated restaurant. However, prices here are refreshingly affordable; at the time of our visit, they started at around $150.

ROOMS FOR ROMANCE

The inn's comfortable and spacious guest rooms are spread among a half dozen or so pueblo-style stucco buildings. A number of rooms have private patios. The furnishings, many of which are as old as the inn, are traditional. The bathrooms boast contemporary appointments.

Rooms 250, 251 (our home for a night), 252, and 187 are recommended, with a caveat: they are located on a side street and do not offer convenient access to the swimming pool and tennis courts. You'll have to walk right through the main lobby or a dark working area to get there. We found rooms 178 and 186, although also very private, to be inconveniently situated as well.

We prefer those rooms situated within the main compound and facing the nicely sculpted and colorful interior lawn and garden area.

ARIZONA INN
2200 East Elm Street
Tucson, AZ 85719
Telephone: (520) 325-1541;
toll-free: (800) 933-1093
www.arizonainn.com

19

THE FACTS

Seven suites, each with private bath. Complimentary
"breakfast in a basket" delivered to each suite. Swimming
pool. Disabled access. Expensive.

GETTING THERE

From Interstate 17, take the Camelback exit and drive east
on Camelback Road. Turn left on Third Avenue and drive
one block to Pasadena Avenue. Turn right and follow to inn.

MARICOPA MANOR
15 West Pasadena Avenue
Phoenix, AZ 85013
Telephone: (602) 274-6302;
toll-free: (800) 292-6403
www.maricopamanor.com

MARICOPA MANOR

Maricopa Manor leads somewhat of a double life. During the work week, guests attracted by the inn's convenient business district location are more apt to be seen clutching briefcases than the hand of a loved one. On Friday afternoons, however, most of the businessfolk depart, making room for smiling, casually dressed couples ready for a romantic weekend in a city that's literally at their feet.

When constructed in the 1920s, this handsome Spanish-style home enjoyed a rural setting a few miles from the center of town. As the city has spread over the years, Maricopa Manor has found itself literally in the shadow of bustling Phoenix, at the edge of a mature, comfortable neighborhood.

Although the pulse of the city beats nearby, the Maricopa Manor estate remains an Eden of sorts, boasting lovely trees, gardens, lush lawns, a swimming pool, and inviting nooks for outdoor relaxing.

Once home to a family that included a dozen children, extended family members, and exchange students, the grand manor and an adjacent home were converted in 1989 into Phoenix's first authorized bed-and-breakfast inn. Since our first visit, ownership of the inn has passed to Jeff Vadheim, a family physician who retired early, trading his medical practice for the role of innkeeper.

ROOMS FOR ROMANCE

Our favorite romantic accommodations are the four "Luxury King Suites," whose high-season (January through March) rates are around $200. Reflections Past is a spacious guest house retreat that includes a living room with a corner gas fireplace flanked by bookcases, a separate bedroom with a king-sized bed, and a private patio. The lavender-hued suite features a great bathroom equipped with a large spa tub and a separate shower.

The Manor Suite, located in the Dos Casas building, has a three-sided gas fireplace that is visible from the bedroom and living areas. The living area is furnished with a pair of love seats, and the bedroom holds a king-sized bed. An Arts-and-Crafts-style décor pervades this spacious hideaway, which also features a bathroom with a large spa tub and a separate shower.

The inn's largest suite is the nicely styled Pasadena Suite, which boasts courtyard views and a private patio. The suite's living room has a couch and a cozy fireplace, and there's a spa tub and a shower in the bathroom.

ROYAL PALMS RESORT AND SPA

5200 East Camelback Road

Phoenix, AZ 85018

Telephone: (602) 840-3610;

toll-free: 800-672-6011

www.royalpalmsresortandspa.com

THE FACTS

One hundred seventeen rooms, each with private bath. Swimming pool and spa. Restaurant and bar. Disabled access. Deluxe.

GETTING THERE

From Phoenix, follow Highway 143 north; take McDowell Exit and turn left. Turn right on Forty-fourth Street and turn right on Camelback Road. Follow for two miles to resort on left.

Like a stately European castle where new additions, nooks, and crannies appear with successive generations, Royal Palms Resort and Spa is a product of a rich history dating back to the Roaring Twenties. It was then that New York shipping magnate Delos Cooke, a nephew of J. P. Morgan, built a luxurious winter home in the grand Spanish colonial style. A decade later, Cooke died and the mansion passed through a number of owners, each of whom put his own imprint on the estate. One even added a chapel.

After World War II, the nine-acre estate opened its doors to travelers, and it's been a Phoenix favorite ever since. A multimillion-dollar restoration in the late 1990s positioned the resort for continued prosperity into the new millennium.

Unlike so many cookie-cutter resorts, Royal Palms accents its varied accommodations with stone fountains, trestle beams, red brick from nineteenth-century Chicago, Mexican stone pavers that date back to the 1600s, and custom tiles. The two of you will feel like guests at a rambling residential estate.

At the time of our travels, the resort's T. Cook's restaurant was offering Mediterranean-style cuisine along with views of Camelback Mountain. There's a poolside grill, round-the-clock room service, and a fitness center. Royal Palms also operates the Alvadora Spa, with nine treatment rooms.

ROOMS FOR ROMANCE

While the sixty-plus Plaza Rooms and Suites (around $400) are definitely serviceable, we recommend you snuggle into one of the resort's stylish Casitas for a more memorable romantic experience. Situated in a secluded citrus garden, the Casitas (around $500) are appointed with custom-designed furniture, iron canopy beds, fireplaces, and French doors that open to patios.

The Deluxe Casitas (mid $500 range), each put together by a different professional design team, are nicer still. The bathrooms in these deluxe units feature walk-in showers. Be sure to check the resort's Web site for specially priced romance packages available during off-season months.

The resort also offers a nine-hundred-square-foot Honeymoon Villa, furnished with a fireplace and a double chaise lounge. A leather-covered tea table here is inscribed, in Spanish, with a phrase that translates to "Give me your hand, Paloma, for this night you will sleep with me."

23

THE FACTS

Ninety-eight suites, each with private bath; many with fireplaces, sunrooms, and private outdoor tubs. Spa. Tennis courts. Fitness center. Four swimming pools. Restaurant and bar. Disabled access. Deluxe.

GETTING THERE

From Phoenix, follow Highway 143 north toward Forty-fourth Street (143 becomes Forty-fourth Street). Continue north and make a slight right onto McDonald Drive. Turn right on Superstition and follow to resort. From Scottsdale Road in Paradise Valley, between Borgata and Scottsdale Fashion Square shopping centers, drive west on McDonald Drive. Follow to resort on left.

SANCTUARY ON CAMELBACK MOUNTAIN
5700 East McDonald Drive
Paradise Valley, AZ 85253
Telephone: (480) 948-2100;
toll-free: (800) 245-2051
www.sanctuaryoncamelback.com

SANCTUARY ON CAMELBACK MOUNTAIN

One of the Phoenix area's newest resorts, Sanctuary on Camelback Mountain has already earned a solid reputation among Southwest-bound romantics. A popular tennis resort in its former life, the Sanctuary tastefully combines traditional Southwest décor with a sleek and chic modern look.

ROOMS FOR ROMANCE

If the two of you lean to the traditional, you'll likely gravitate toward the resort's redesigned Southwestern-style Mountain Casitas. These accommodations, terraced into craggy Camelback Mountain, feature rock fireplaces and glass sunrooms. The Mountain Casita Suites are particularly romantic.

Other guests will prefer the two-dozen trendy and spacious Luxury Spa Casitas, which have generated the most buzz among travelers and the travel media. These spacious accommodations surround the swimming pool and the resort spa and are decorated in a minimalist style, with polished concrete floors, king-sized platform beds heaped with upscale linens, bright colors, impressive lighting systems, and electronic gadgetry. The private outdoor "steeping tubs" are a particularly decadent romantic amenity and reason alone to settle into one of these accommodations.

Travelers should be advised that the views here, like the accommodations, vary. Some rooms, particularly the spa suites, face a residential area of Paradise Valley while others offer inspirational mountain vistas. The dozen casitas located on the west side of the resort's spa offer the best views. Be sure to let the reservation staff know if a view is important to you.

Of particular note is the resort's Sanctuary Spa, a luxurious facility offering eleven treatment rooms, an indoor-outdoor treatment facility, a movement studio, a lap pool, and a Zen meditation garden. The resort's infinity pool is reportedly the largest in Arizona.

The resort's popular restaurant serves American food with an Asian twist, along with a fabulous view.

High-season nightly rates start at around $500. Summer rates are substantially less.

GOLD CANYON GOLF RESORT
6100 South Kings Ranch Road
Apache Junction, AZ 85218
Telephone toll-free: (800) 624-6445
www.gcgr.com

THE FACTS

Eighty rooms, each with private bath and indoor or outdoor fireplace; many with tubs or spas for two. Golf course, tennis courts, swimming pool, restaurant, and lounge. Disabled access. No minimum stay requirement. Expensive to deluxe.

GETTING THERE

From Phoenix, drive east on Highway 60 (Superstition Freeway). Take Kings Ranch Road exit and drive one mile to resort on left. Resort is approximately forty minutes from Sky Harbor Airport.

GOLD CANYON GOLF RESORT

Forget the legendary Lost Dutchman's Mine, purportedly hidden in the adjacent Superstition Mountains. Gold Canyon Ranch is the X mark on our Arizona treasure map.

This desert retreat, so close yet so far from the fast pace of Phoenix, is a favorite of metropolitan-area couples in-the-know looking for a convenient romantic getaway. The stunning whitewashed Spanish-style casitas are set against craggy hills, from which the city's distant shimmering lights can be seen at night. Since our first visit, many of the resort's accommodations have been sold to time-share guests. However, about eighty suites are still available to the public.

Also worthy of note are the resort's impeccably tended grounds, which are profuse with mesquite and several types of cacti, including aging saguaros, spiny strawberries, Arizona barrels, and prickly pears.

ROOMS FOR ROMANCE

The Gold Canyon casitas are some of the Phoenix area's most romantically equipped. All have wood-burning fireplaces, and a healthy number of the accommodations come with private indoor or outdoor tubs or spas for two.

As if our Gold Canyon casita didn't offer enough romantic potential, our visit coincided with Valentine's Day. Toasting the end of the day from our indoor spa in front of a flickering fire, we were easy prey for Cupid.

For romantic getaways, we give our highest recommendation to the rooms with spacious private spas (around $300), all of which have private patios. We particularly like the Superior Casitas, which feature big indoor spas, king-sized beds, fireplaces, and patios. The inside Spa Casitas have smaller but spacious spa tubs, fireplaces, and two queen-sized beds. For those who enjoy the sun and moon, we recommend the Outside Spa Casitas, which are furnished with king-sized beds. Guests should be advised that some of the tantalizing outdoor spas are visible from adjacent walkways, so swimsuits are de rigueur.

The rates noted above are for the resort's high season, from January through mid-May. Summer rates for spa rooms are less expensive.

27

DAYTIME DIVERSIONS

At the GRAND CANYON's south entrance, you'll find an IMAX theater that displays the canyon's wonders on a seven-story screen. Two of the most popular hiking trails, Bright Angel and South Kaibab, start near Grand Canyon Village.

FLAGSTAFF visitors might want to check out the Anasazi Indian ruins at the Wupatki National Monument, thirty-five miles north of town. The Snowbowl ski area is located fourteen miles south of Flagstaff.

Discover the natural forces of SEDONA through a vortex tour or an Indian petroglyph hike conducted by Earth Wisdom Tours, (520) 282-4714. Those conspicuous pink jeeps you see around the area take visitors on year-round off-road tours of Sedona's Red Rock country and the Coconino National Forest, (800) 873-3662. If you'd prefer to see Sedona from a saddle, call Kachina Stables at (520) 282-7252. Sedona's popular Tlaquepaque Arts and Crafts Village shopping complex is on Highway 179 at the Oak Creek Bridge.

Visitors to PINETOP have access to the White Mountain trail system, whose 180 miles of bike, hiking, and horse trails connect five parks.

TABLES FOR TWO

Cucina Rustica, 7000 Highway 179, SEDONA
René at Tlaquepaque, 336 Highway 179, SEDONA
Savannah's, 2611 West Highway 89A, SEDONA
Heartline Café, 1610 West Highway 89A, SEDONA
The Rose, 234 South Cortez Street, PRESCOTT
Phineas T's, 1450 E. White Mountain Boulevard, PINETOP

NORTHERN ARIZONA

THE FACTS

Eight cabins, each with bath, kitchen, and fireplace. Smoking is not permitted. No disabled access. Two-night minimum stay required during weekends; three- to four-night minimum during holiday periods. Expensive.

GETTING THERE

From Highway 260 one mile east of Pinetop, turn north on Bucksprings Road. Drive a half mile and turn left on Sky Hi Road. Drive two miles to Sierra Springs Drive, and stay to right for ranch entrance. Ranch is approximately 190 miles from Phoenix and 185 miles from Tucson.

SIERRA SPRINGS RANCH
101 Sky Hi Road
Pinetop, AZ 85935
Telephone: (928) 369-3900;
toll-free: (800) 492-4059
www.sierraspringsranch.com

SIERRA SPRINGS RANCH

In assembling each of our *Weekend for Two* volumes, we've made at least one romantic discovery that we would have preferred to keep all to ourselves. In the Southwest, Sierra Springs Ranch is one of those special places.

If you believe that a visit to the Pinetop-Lakeside region necessarily includes motels, traffic, and pizza parlors, a weekend at this remote seventy-six-acre all-season resort will enrich the two of you with a soul-stirring new perspective.

The ranch consists of a collection of new and restored cabins that sit under ponderosa pines at the edge of a wide meadow, which sparkles with snow in winter before turning a luxuriant green in spring. The property also includes private lakes, a fitness center, a sauna, hiking and ski trails, a gazebo, and a tennis court.

The lack of an on-site restaurant might tempt some visitors to venture into town for dinner, but many guests choose to take advantage of the barbecues and kitchen facilities with tableware, savoring an intimate home-cooked meal under the pines.

ROOMS FOR ROMANCE

Depending on the cabin, your Sierra Springs Ranch hideaway might feature cedar paneling, pine log walls, an antique clawfoot tub, or a modern shower. Each, however, is richly appointed with comfortable furniture, soft carpeting, and a well-equipped kitchen. Most of the cabins have multiple bedrooms, making Sierra Springs Ranch a great destination if you want to get away but can't secure a babysitter. Some of the larger cabins can even accommodate the babysitter.

Couples will cherish a night or two in the Honeymoon Cabin (around $200), a nine-hundred-square-foot one-bedroom charmer with a king-sized four-poster bed and a sunny bathroom, where an antique bathtub with a hand-held shower attachment sits in a windowed corner.

The Santa Fe (around $200) is an even larger cabin with two bedrooms. The master bedroom contains a king-sized bed, and the other holds two twins.

The refurbished Barn Cottage (low $200 range), another spacious and delightful accommodation, holds two upstairs bedrooms with two private bathrooms. The Cheyenne and the Pueblo Lodge are the two other multibedroom units; these are best suited for larger groups but can also accommodate couples.

PLEASANT STREET INN

142 South Pleasant Street
Prescott, AZ 86303
Telephone: (928) 445-4774;
toll-free: (877) 226-7128
www.pleasantbandb.com

THE FACTS

Four rooms, each with private bath. Complimentary full breakfast served at communal table. Two-night minimum stay required during holiday periods. Moderate.

GETTING THERE

From Interstate 17, exit at Cordes Junction onto Highway 69 and follow northwest for thirty-three miles to Prescott. In Prescott, turn left on Highway 89, which becomes Gurley Street. Turn left on Pleasant Street and follow to inn on right, at the corner of Pleasant and Goodwin Streets.

PLEASANT STREET INN

During a tour of the residential sections of this former Arizona territorial capital city, we made quite a romantic discovery behind the door of a well-tended turn-of-the-century home. Expecting that the vintage exterior would be mirrored inside, we were pleasantly surprised to find a completely updated, enlarged, and very comfortable interior with moderately priced guest rooms.

Relocated a decade or so ago to a shady corner of the aptly named Pleasant Street, just three blocks from the historic courthouse plaza, the old home has been adopted by resident innkeeper Jeanne Watkins, who treats her guests to bright, spacious rooms with rich traditional furnishings, wall-to-wall carpeting, ceiling fans, and private bathrooms.

Outside, an inviting front deck is arranged with cozy wicker furniture, providing guests with a quiet place to relax after the three-block walk from Prescott's historic Courthouse Square and downtown shops.

ROOMS FOR ROMANCE

Our highest recommendation is given to the Pine View Suite (mid $100 range), an elegant two-room accommodation on the second floor. A comfortable bay-windowed sitting room boasts a pretty blue-tiled woodburning fireplace and a sofa, and the adjacent bedroom holds a king-sized bed. The bright bathroom has double sinks.

Our other romantic favorite is the Terrace Suite (mid $100 range), the only guest room on the first floor. It consists of a separate sitting room with a couch and a chair, a private covered deck, and a windowless bedroom with a queen-sized bed. The small bathroom holds a tub-and-shower combination.

Offered for just over $100 per night, the second-floor Garden Room faces the front of the property and is appointed with wicker furnishings and a queen-sized bed. The small bathroom has a tiny sink and a shower stall.

Prescott (low $100 range) is another second-floor corner room, offering a king-sized bed and views of the distant mountains. Traveling romantics should note that this room's spacious and private bath is across the hall.

THE FACTS

Eleven rooms, each with private bath; four with fireplaces. Complimentary full breakfast served at communal tables. Swimming pool. Disabled access. Two-night minimum stay required during weekends; three-night minimum during holiday periods. Moderate to expensive.

GETTING THERE

From Interstate 17, take exit 298/Sedona and follow Highway 179 for eight miles. Turn left on Bell Rock Boulevard (third traffic light). Follow for one block and turn right on Canyon Circle Drive. Inn is on right.

CANYON VILLA BED AND BREAKFAST

Long after we had departed Sedona, the surreal view from Canyon Villa's Spanish Bayonet Room (around $300) lingered in our memory. Not only does this entrancing room overlook majestic Bell Rock, a dramatic sandstone landmark, the view, as well as an in-room fireplace, can be savored through French doors from the in-room whirlpool tub as well as from the cozy king-sized bed.

And don't despair if Spanish Bayonet is booked during your visit to Sedona. There are other similarly impressive accommodations at this romantic hideaway tucked into a residential area in the Village of Oak Creek, a short drive from Sedona proper.

Even those who are not usually attracted to lobbies and living rooms during a romantic weekend away will be drawn to Canyon Villa's common area, with its high ceilings and hanging fans and a big see-through fireplace. There's a small library with white oak floors, and an expanse of windows overlooks the swimming pool. An outdoor fireplace stands next to the pool, and Bell Rock and Courthouse Butte loom dramatically in the distance.

A plus for romantics is the inn's policy of not booking weddings and group events, which can sometimes intrude on the experience of other guests.

ROOMS FOR ROMANCE

A great romantic choice is Strawberry Cactus (mid $200 range), a corner room with vivid blue carpeting, a king-sized bed, and a small balcony with a grand view. The bathroom holds a whirlpool tub-and-shower combination.

The other second-floor room with a fireplace, Ocotillo (around $300), features Southwestern décor, a love seat, and a king-sized bed. The view from this corner room is outstanding.

The two best rooms on the ground floor are the western-themed Mariposa Room and the king-bedded Claret Cup (around $300), which is more traditionally styled. These rooms have private view patios, gas fireplaces, and single-sized whirlpool tubs; Mariposa also has a separate shower. Desert Daisy has a king-sized bed and is offered in the low $200 range.

The Agave Room (high $100 range), which features a walled patio, is very private, but it lacks the dramatic views of the other rooms. This is the only room without a whirlpool tub.

CANYON VILLA BED AND BREAKFAST
125 Canyon Circle Drive
Sedona, AZ 86351
Telephone: (520) 284-1226;
toll-free: (800) 453-1166
www.canyonvilla.com

ADOBE VILLAGE GRAHAM INN
150 Canyon Circle Drive
Sedona, AZ 86351
Telephone: (520) 284-1425;
toll-free: (800) 228-1425
www.sedonasfinest.com

THE FACTS

Ten rooms, each with private bath and television with videocassette player; four have fireplaces; three have spa tubs for two. Complimentary full breakfast served at communal table, at tables for two, or in your room. Swimming pool and free rental bikes. No handicapped access. Two-night minimum stay required during weekends; three-night minimum during some holiday periods. Moderate to deluxe.

GETTING THERE

From Interstate 17, take exit 298/Sedona and follow Highway 179 for eight miles. Turn left on Bell Rock Boulevard (third traffic light). Follow for two blocks to inn on right at corner of Bell Rock Boulevard and Canyon Circle Drive.

ADOBE VILLAGE GRAHAM INN

In our initial planning for this romantic guide to the Southwest, we envisioned one, maybe two, destinations in Sedona. As we toured the area, however, every bend in the road revealed a new and enticing panorama, and each of the inns we visited offered an inviting experience.

Located a few miles south of Sedona in the Village of Oak Creek, Adobe Village Graham Inn is one of those off-the-beaten-track discoveries that we felt compelled to share. Among the smallest of our recommended Sedona-area hideaways, Graham Inn is situated in a residential area and might easily be mistaken for a private home.

Guests are pampered with amenities like videocassette players, custom tile, and spa tubs for two in a contemporary Southwest atmosphere. Views of towering sandstone pinnacles with names like Satan's Arch and Wildhorse Mesa are offered from some guest rooms as well as from the backyard swimming pool and spa.

ROOMS FOR ROMANCE

New since our first visit are four super-sized, ultra-romantic suites. Among these, Lonesome Dove Villa (mid $400) has a king-sized bed and a large sitting area with a stone fireplace. The stunning bathroom holds a freestanding spa tub for two reminiscent of a hot tub, and a stove-styled fireplace. There's also a walk-in shower.

The log walls, beamed ceiling, and expansive river-rock fireplace of the Wilderness Villa will have the two of you feeling as if you're snuggled away in a cozy mountain cabin. However, we've never experienced a cabin with a bathroom like the one here. It features a walk-in shower with a waterfall, a spa tub for two set in stone, and another stone fireplace.

We enjoyed a night in the inn's Sedona Suite (around $400), a favorite among honeymooners. The suite boasts a fabulous bath with two vanities, a spa tub for two and steam shower combination, and a fireplace. The bedroom holds a king-sized Taos-style bed and a television with a DVD player. (The inn maintains a sizable movie collection.) The living room has a woodburning fireplace, while the private outdoor patio faces Satan's Arch and is furnished with a table and chairs.

ADOBE GRAND VILLAS

If we gave an award for the "most romantic" of our Southwestern places of the heart, the Adobe Village Graham Inn's sister property would take away the prize—not to mention our breath.

New in 2004, Adobe Grand Villas take Sedona's romantic lodging options to a whole new level. Situated around an inviting swimming pool, five 2-story buildings contain fifteen of the most sumptuous accommodations we've discovered anywhere in the country. They're also quite spacious, the smallest measuring over eight hundred square feet in size. At the time of our travels, weekend rates started in the mid $800 range.

The villas are located at 35 Hozoni Drive.

THE FACTS

Sixteen rooms, each with private bath, fireplace, and spa tub for one or two. Complimentary full breakfast served at tables for two in dining room or at outdoor terrace tables. Spa. Disabled access. Two-night minimum stay required during weekends. Expensive.

GETTING THERE

From Interstate 17, take exit 287 (Route 260) and drive west for twelve miles to Cottonwood. Turn right on Highway 89A and drive north for fourteen miles toward Sedona. Just past second traffic light, turn left on Tortilla Drive and another left at first stop sign on Southwest Drive. Take an immediate right onto Hozoni Drive. Inn is on left.

CASA SEDONA

Designed by a protégé of Frank Lloyd Wright, this elegant Southwestern-style inn occupies a particularly scenic spot near the new Adobe Grand Villas (see separate listing). Guests are treated to enchanting views of the landscape and rugged mountains. Mongollon Rim, visible from many of the rooms, changes color throughout the day as the sun rises and sets. Other impressive formations visible from the property bear names like Lizard Head, Chimney Rock, and Coffee Pot Rock.

The inn's rural setting offers visiting couples the option of setting off on day hikes just a hop, skip, and jump from the Casa Sedona property. If trekking isn't on your itinerary, simply sit on the spacious patio under century-old junipers and soak up the atmosphere and the soothing sounds of a water fountain. And the Sedona shops are just a short drive away.

ROOMS FOR ROMANCE

With red-rock views, a fireplace, and spa tubs offered with every room, it's difficult to pick favorites here. However, the luscious Sunset Suite (upper $100 range) is one of the inn's most popular accommodations. Facing the rear of the property, the suite holds rocking armchairs and a separate shower, as well as the aforementioned romantic amenities.

Trickster Den (mid $200 range) is a corner room from which majestic Thunder Mountain is visible. This room, designed in a whimsical style by famed mime Robert Shields, has a large spa tub, a corner fireplace, and a terrace that affords pretty sunset vistas.

Sweeping red-rock views from three directions— and even from the bathroom—are reason alone to book a weekend for two in Hopi (mid $200 range). Anasazi and Navajo (mid $200 range) have private sunset-view terraces, and Hozoni has a private deck.

Early risers will particularly enjoy Safari (mid $200 range), which features a handsome African motif and a bedside fireplace, along with gorgeous sunrise vistas and great morning light.

CASA SEDONA
55 Hozoni Drive
Sedona, AZ 86336
Telephone: (928) 282-2938;
toll-free: (800) 525-3756
www.casasedona.com

L'Auberge De Sedona

301 L'Auberge Lane
Sedona, AZ 86336
Telephone: (928) 282-7131;
toll-free: (800) 272-6777
www.lauberge.com

THE FACTS

Fifty-eight rooms (plus forty-one rooms in Orchard building), each with private bath. Swimming pool and restaurant. Disabled access. Two-night minimum stay required during weekends and holiday periods. Moderate to deluxe.

GETTING THERE

From Interstate 17 (two hours from Phoenix), exit at Highway 179 and drive north fifteen miles to Sedona. At intersection of Highways 179 and 89A, turn right onto Highway 89A. Immediately on right is Cedars Resort, and next to it is a small street sign for L'Auberge Lane. Follow lane to right and into resort.

Visitors to L'Auberge de Sedona who are unaccustomed to living in the lap of sinful luxury will likely feel the same guilty pleasure that comes with sliding behind the wheel of an expensive sports car or diving into a bowl of premium ice cream. Lolling in our luxurious room, floating in the pool while gazing at the distant red rugged landscape, and dining by the serene creek, we wondered whether anyone was really worthy of such an experience.

Set along Oak Creek amid trees and gardens, the resort engenders a feeling of delightful seclusion, although the bustling Tlaquepaque Arts and Crafts Village is only a short walk away. We'd guess that most Sedona visitors aren't even aware of this delicious canyon resort hidden just off the main road.

Offering the most varied accommodations of our recommended Sedona properties, L'Auberge tempts couples with a menu of choices that ranges from cozy creekside cabins to mouthwatering hillside rooms with panoramas of red bluffs and spires.

ROOMS FOR ROMANCE

We'll start with the cottages, an enchanting collection of more than two dozen European-style gems clustered along or near the rushing creek. These have been redecorated since our first visit, and all have hardwood floors, beds with dark cherry headboards, leather sofas, fireplaces, and porches.

We spent a warm summer night in cottage 2, set on a grassy knoll under a canopy of trees and overlooking melodious Oak Creek. Our covered front porch held two cushioned pine-log chairs. Inside was a spacious living room with a fireplace, a couch, a table and chairs, a television, and a CD player. The two bedrooms each held a queen-sized bed.

Cottages 5 and 6 are the most remote of the creek-facing units. Cottages 1 through 4 face the creek and lawn. At the upper part of the property, cottages 15 through 19 occupy a sandy creekside spot. One-bedroom cottages are offered in the high $400 range; two-bedroom cottages fetch tariffs in the mid $500 range. Rates are considerably lower from mid-November through February.

Another option is the European-style lodge, situated near the center of the property. This attractive building houses a dramatic lobby and conference rooms, as well as several guest rooms (low $200 range to around $300) with king-sized beds.

If you're interested in red-rock romance, we suggest a room in the Orchards building, which sits on the hillside above the cottages and lodge. Connected to the canyon floor by a funicular, the Orchards consists of nicely appointed rooms (upper $100 range), some with fireplaces and each with a balcony or patio offering dramatic mountain vistas. Set at street level, the Orchards provides direct and quick access to Sedona shops.

THE LODGE AT SEDONA

125 Kallof Place
Sedona, AZ 86336
Telephone: (928) 204-1942;
toll-free: (800) 619-4467
www.lodgeatsedona.com

THE FACTS

Fourteen rooms, each with private bath. Complimentary full breakfast served at tables for two and four or in your room. Walking labyrinth. Fitness center and swimming pool privileges. Disabled access. Two-night minimum stay required during weekends and holiday periods. Expensive to deluxe.

GETTING THERE

From Interstate 17 (two hours from Phoenix), exit at Highway 179 and drive north fifteen miles to Sedona. In downtown Sedona, turn left on Highway 89A and follow for two miles. Turn left on Kallof Place and follow to inn.

THE LODGE AT SEDONA

Built in 1959 for one of Sedona's first doctors, his wife, and their dozen children, the Lodge at Sedona still bears some resemblance to a comfortable family home. Tucked away in a nice neighborhood and almost hidden behind fragrant pine trees, the inn and its three acres of landscaped gardens serve up a variety of inviting public and private spaces, as well as a very friendly tone set by innkeeper Shelley Wachal, who even extends a welcome to pets.

Said to have been inspired by the architecture of Frank Lloyd Wright, the lodge blends Mission styling with a warm, inviting atmosphere. Three guest lounges accentuated with river rock, local red brick, and slate compete for the attention of guests. Red-rock vistas serve as a dramatic backdrop, and the lodge's circular stone labyrinth provides guests with a dose of meditative solitude and a path to what many believe is a clearer state of mind.

ROOMS FOR ROMANCE

If the two of you are looking for the ultimate romantic accommodation, look no further than the Red Rock Crossing Suite (low $300 range), a luxury retreat with an indoor spa tub for two as well as an outdoor hot tub. Boasting a king-sized bed and a sitting area, the suite also features twin massage showers, two stereos, and a huge red-rock fireplace.

Red-rock views, twin patios, and a private outdoor hot tub are among the romantic attractions of the Mission Grande Suite (around $300). You'll also enjoy the large fireplace, king-sized bed, sitting area, and the bathroom with a spa tub.

Guests in the Star Gazer Suite (mid $200 range) enjoy a large cedar deck with an outdoor shower. There's also a cozy corner fireplace, a spa tub, and a triple-mist shower.

Privacy seekers head to the secluded Copper Canyon Suite (mid $200 range), which features a timber cottage décor. The lovely deck is surrounded by piñon trees and affords great red-rock views.

Offered for the relatively bargain tariff of around $200, the Mystic Mountain Room is a second-floor room with a reading nook and a fireplace. Dream Weaver, offered in the same price range, features great red-rock views, an antique stove fireplace, and a cozy window seat. These rooms have queen-sized beds.

THE FACTS

One hundred sixty-two rooms and suites, each with private bath. Complimentary orange juice and newspaper delivered to your room each morning. Full-service spa. Swimming pools, tennis courts, a golf course, and a croquet course. Two local golf courses. Restaurants and lounges. Disabled access. Smoking allowed. Two-night minimum stay required during weekends; three-night minimum during holiday periods. Deluxe.

GETTING THERE

From Interstate 17 (two hours from Phoenix), exit at Highway 179 and drive north fifteen miles to Sedona. In downtown Sedona, turn left on Highway 89A and follow for three miles. Turn right on Dry Creek Road and follow to Boynton Canyon Road. Turn right and follow to resort. Office is on left.

ENCHANTMENT RESORT

Those who require proof that a magical energy pervades the Sedona area need only experience Enchantment Resort to become, well, enchanted. On our private east-facing patio, the two of us sat silent and awestruck as a setting winter sun painted looming canyon walls with a changing palette of hypnotic hues. Strolling onto the darkened patio after dinner, we were greeted with another masterpiece: the dazzling night sky.

During our Sedona sojourns, we've not discovered a retreat that better showcases the region's mountain majesty than Enchantment Resort. If you're only able to stay, heaven forbid, one night in Sedona, we recommend you spend it here.

The resort has a Sedona address, but it's actually situated about five scenic miles from town, hidden in rugged Boynton Canyon and presided over by trees and towering sandstone walls. It's a full-service destination, offering a dozen tennis courts, four swimming pools, outdoor spas, golf, a croquet court, a fabulous new spa, and multiple restaurants. There's also an outdoor deck on the roof of the clubhouse for panoramic views of the twinkling heavens. Hiking trails along the canyon walls lead to ancient ruins and caves.

ROOMS FOR ROMANCE

Dotting the seventy-acre property are dozens of Southwestern-style casitas, most housing three units each. There is a range of lodging options, the least expensive of which are Casita Studios (around $400). These feature living rooms with log-beamed ceilings, kiva fireplaces, queen-sized beds, and kitchenettes.

We spent a memorable night in room 340, which holds two queen-sized beds. The well-equipped bathroom has double sinks, and we found the elevated patio very private, providing the two of us with impressive views of the canyon walls.

Offered for around $500, Casita Junior Suites are spacious accommodations equipped with ample living and bedroom areas, kiva fireplaces, and large bathrooms with oval soaking tubs and separate showers. These also feature private decks.

At the time of our travels, the resort offered a variety of specially priced packages, among them a romance package that included a candle-lit dinner and spa treatments.

ENCHANTMENT RESORT
525 Boynton Canyon Road
Sedona, AZ 86336
Telephone: (928) 282-2900;
toll-free: (800) 826-4180
www.enchantmentresort.com

45

THE FACTS

Eleven rooms, each with private bath, gas fireplace, and whirlpool tub; eight with spa tubs for two. Complimentary full breakfast served at tables for two. Complimentary afternoon and evening refreshments. Two-night minimum stay required during weekends and holidays. Smoking allowed only in certain outdoor areas. Disabled access. Expensive.

GETTING THERE

From Interstate 17 (two hours from Phoenix), take exit 298 and follow Highway 179 north approximately fourteen miles to heart of Sedona. Inn is adjacent to Highway 179 on left.

THE INN ON OAK CREEK

While many Sedona inns can claim enchanting red-rock views, there are few that complement mountain views with soothing water vistas. From its romantic perch above Oak Creek, the Inn on Oak Creek has all the ingredients for a memorable Sedona stay.

An art gallery at the time of our initial travels, the Inn on Oak Creek is among Sedona's newest romantic retreats. And its creators, the Morris family, have added just the right touches to quickly enchant the hearts of the many visitors who've made this a northern Arizona favorite.

ROOMS FOR ROMANCE

Made for special moments, Angler's Retreat (high $200 range) is a large and dramatic upstairs corner room that looks over and along the creek toward picturesque distant red-rock formations. This honeymoon-worthy room, furnished with a king-sized bed and a spa tub for two, has great window exposure, as well as a fireplace and a private deck overlooking the water.

Another romantic favorite is Rose Arbor (mid $200 range), a corner room decorated in a country floral theme and offering a spa tub for two, a wicker love seat, a fireplace, and inspirational creek and mountain views.

Rested Rooster (mid $200 range) boasts French provincial farmhouse décor and is equipped with a spa tub for two overlooking the creek. This room also has a private creek-view deck, a fireplace, two chairs, and a queen-sized bed.

The Native American–themed Trading Post (around $200) offers red-rock views from a queen-sized lodgepole bed. This handsome room also has a spa tub for two.

Homestead Hearts, Bunkhouse, and Apple Orchard have single spa tubs; Hollywood West overlooks a park.

THE INN ON OAK CREEK
556 Highway 179
Sedona, AZ 86336
Telephone: (928) 282-0696;
toll-free: (800) 499-7896
www.innonoakcreek.com

THE INN AT 410

410 North Leroux Street
Flagstaff, AZ 86001
Telephone: (928) 774-0088;
toll-free: (800) 774-2008
www.inn410.com

THE FACTS

Nine rooms, each with private bath and gas fireplace; three with spa tubs for two. Complimentary full breakfast served in dining room or continental breakfast delivered to your room. Disabled access. Two-night minimum stay required during weekends from April through October. Moderate to expensive.

GETTING THERE

Interstate 17 north becomes Milton Road in Flagstaff. In downtown Flagstaff, follow northbound Milton as it curves right and becomes Santa Fe Avenue (Route 66). Turn left on Leroux Street and follow four blocks up hill to inn on right.

THE INN AT 410

In the early 1970s, visitors to 410 North Leroux Street were more likely looking for a beer bust or a toga party than a quiet romantic overnight interlude. These days, the atmosphere at this former fraternity house is considerably more sedate, the rousing choruses of "Louie Louie" having been replaced by the crackling of a fire and hushed conversations among traveling couples. Visitors aren't even disturbed by televisions or telephones.

This tidy, well-preserved, two-story century-old brick home served as a family residence for several generations. After its stint as a Northern Arizona University frat house, the property was converted into apartments. It became an inn in the early 1990s. Gordon and Carol Watkins are the current owners-innkeepers.

Situated in a clean and quiet neighborhood only a couple of blocks above Flagstaff's downtown shops and restaurants, the gray-and-white inn has sunny and inviting public areas and a canvas-covered patio for outdoor relaxing. A full breakfast is served at a communal table and tables for two, or a continental breakfast can be delivered to your room.

ROOMS FOR ROMANCE

Each offered for around $200, the Southwest Room and the Tea Room are without question the inn's most romantic accommodations. The Southwest is a grand first-floor suite with brick walls, French doors opening to a bathroom with an elegant spa tub for two, a white plaster fireplace, a couch, and a queen-sized Taos-style bed.

The home's original mahogany paneling is one of two intriguing features of the Tea Room. The other is a collection of teapots. This room has a love seat at the foot of a king-sized bed, a pair of cushy chairs set before a lovely window, a fireplace, and a bathroom with a spa tub for two.

A plush romantic love seat and a raised woodstove-style fireplace are the centerpieces of Monet's Garden (around $200), a romantic retreat with a spa-tub-for-two nook and a private outdoor entry.

For bargain hunters, the small-but-sweet Sonoran Serenade was being offered in the mid $100 range at the time of our last visit. This colorful room is furnished with a pretty queen-sized iron bed draped in Mexican lace, and offers a fireplace and a private bathroom.

49

THE FACTS

Seventy-eight rooms, each with private bath. Restaurant and lounge. Dinner reservations advised. Disabled access. No minimum stay requirement. Moderate to deluxe.

GETTING THERE

From Phoenix, follow Interstate 17 north to Flagstaff. In Flagstaff, drive west on Interstate 40 to Williams. From Williams, drive north on Highways 64/180 to Grand Canyon Village; hotel is on right.

EL TOVAR HOTEL

Considered the jewel of the Grand Canyon, El Tovar Hotel has been treating visitors to memorable canyon vistas and vacations since just after the turn of the twentieth century.

Inspired by European hunting lodges, the rustic yet stately hostelry was named in memory of Don Pedro de Tovar, a Spanish explorer who happened upon this beautiful spot long ago. Today, it's a Registered National Historic Landmark.

The hotel's interior and exterior architecture is stunning. Native stone, massive beams, and log walls are used extensively throughout the public areas. Fireplaces abound. Two of the favorite gathering spots are El Tovar Lounge and its outdoor lounge deck.

ROOMS FOR ROMANCE

El Tovar, which offers the canyon's most deluxe overnight experience, underwent an extensive renovation in 2005. The hotel classifies its rooms as standard double-bed rooms (low $100 range); standard queen-bed rooms (low to mid $100 range); deluxe (mid $100 range); and suites, which run to around $300. Deluxe rooms have sitting areas while suites have separate sitting rooms.

For romantic getaways, we recommend either deluxe rooms or suites. Three suites have balconies with canyon views. Other rooms may have a peek of the canyon, but since you can't request a specific room number, it's the luck of the draw.

EL TOVAR HOTEL

South Rim, Grand Canyon
c/o Grand Canyon National Park Lodges
P.O. Box 699
Grand Canyon, AZ 86023
Telephone: (928) 638-2631;
toll-free: (888) 297-2757
www.grandcanyonlodges.com

THE FACTS

Seventy-one rooms and cabins, most with private baths and queen-sized beds. Two restaurants, lounge, and gift shop. Disabled access. Open all year. No minimum stay requirement. Moderate.

GETTING THERE

From Phoenix, follow Interstate 17 north to Flagstaff. In Flagstaff, drive west on Interstate 40 to Williams. From Williams, drive north on Highways 64/180 to Grand Canyon Village; lodge is on right just past El Tovar.

BRIGHT ANGEL LODGE AND CABINS

Perched on the south rim in the shadow of the more famous El Tovar, Bright Angel Lodge is a less-expensive Grand Canyon lodging alternative and offers a more rustic experience.

The second oldest lodge on the south rim, Bright Angel includes not only standard guest rooms but a collection of popular rim-hugging cabins that can be yours for a relatively bargain price.

ROOMS FOR ROMANCE

Many of the little cabins (around $100) are situated dramatically close to the canyon's edge, while others have less-inspiring locations. Some of the cabins even have fireplaces. Rim-hugging cabins carry affordable tariffs in the low $100 range.

Traveling romantics need to keep in mind that some of the cabins are old, rustic, plain, and simple. It's only a step or two away from a camping experience, so don't expect the Ritz. Also, the popular canyon-rim walkway skirts this property, and there usually are lots of camera- and ice-cream-cone-toting tourists around during the daytime. That being said, the cabins provide a distinctive experience, particularly for couples who enjoy nature.

Compared to our other featured destinations, the anonymous lodge building is architecturally lackluster, and the rooms can best be described as standard. However, some do have great views of the Grand Canyon. Lodge rooms with private baths are offered for less than $100.

BRIGHT ANGEL LODGE AND CABINS
South Rim, Grand Canyon
c/o Grand Canyon National Park Lodges
P.O. Box 699
Grand Canyon, AZ 86023
Telephone: (928) 638-2631;
toll-free: (888) 297-2757
www.grandcanyonlodges.com

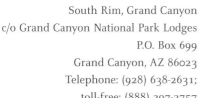

DAYTIME DIVERSIONS

Every October, the streets of LAS CRUCES heat up with
the popular Enchilada Festival, a wild three-day-long fiesta
during which the world's largest enchilada is created.
Two miles away from Las Cruces is MESILLA, a carefully
preserved historic New Mexican town with galleries, restaurants, and shops.

The famous Santa Fe Opera, held in an open-air
auditorium seven miles north of SANTA FE, typically runs
from July through late August. For summer daytime
excitement, ask your Santa Fe innkeeper about Rio
Grande or Rio Chama rafting trips. During the winter
months, locals and visitors head for the Santa Fe Ski Area
in the SANGRE DE CRISTO MOUNTAINS about sixteen
miles northeast of Santa Fe. Santa Fe's Museum Hill is
home to the impressive Museum of International Folk Art
and the Wheelwright Museum of the American Indian.
In the mood for a margarita? Drop by the Cowgirl Hall of
Fame lounge on South Guadalupe Street.

The TAOS area, famous for skiing as well as art,
is the home of Taos Ski Valley, with some of the nation's
most challenging slopes. The Taos Pueblo, just two miles
from town, is the largest multistoried pueblo structure in
the United States. Residents conduct informal tours for
daytime visitors. Taos Plaza, in the heart of town, is surrounded by interesting shops and eateries. The Kit Carson
Home and Museum and the Millicent Rogers Museum are
each worth a visit. And you won't travel more than a few
steps in Taos without stumbling on an art gallery. At last
count, there were around eighty.

In ALBUQUERQUE, we recommend a stroll through
Old Town and the thrilling two-and-a-half-mile ride on the
nation's longest aerial tram on SANDÍA PEAK.

Those romantic New Mexican Christmas celebrations,
when flickering *farolitos* and *luminarias* light the crisp
night sky, generally run from early December into January.

TABLES FOR TWO

Way Out West, 1720 Avienda de Mesilla, LAS CRUCES
Seasons, Mountain Road at San Felipe, ALBUQUERQUE
Antiquity, Romero Street at South Plaza, ALBUQUERQUE
Rancho de San Juan, Highway 285, GALISTEO
Geronimo, 724 Canyon Road, SANTA FE
The Compound, 653 Canyon Road, SANTA FE
Paul's, 72 West Marcy Street, SANTA FE
La Casa Sena Restaurant, 125 East Palace Avenue, SANTA FE
Santacafe, 231 Washington Avenue, SANTA FE
Joseph's Table, South Plaza, TAOS
Lambert's, 309 Paseo del Pueblo Sur, TAOS

NEW MEXICO

THE FACTS
Twenty rooms, each with private bath. Complimentary breakfast served at large communal table, tables for two, or in your room. Art gallery. Disabled access. Smoking allowed. Two-night minimum stay during holiday periods. Moderate.

GETTING THERE
From southbound Interstate 25, take the Lohman exit and turn right. Follow for approximately five miles and turn left on Alameda Boulevard. Inn is on right.

LUNDEEN INN OF THE ARTS
618 South Alameda Boulevard
Las Cruces, NM 88005
Telephone: (505) 526-3326;
toll-free: (888) 526-3326
www.innofthearts.com

LUNDEEN INN OF THE ARTS

Jerry and Linda Lundeen run what you might call a full-service inn for romantics. Not only does the couple set the stage with their romantic décor, Jerry can write a personal marriage ceremony and pronounce you husband and wife on the spot.

A North Dakota native reared on an Indian reservation, Jerry is a lay minister (as well as an architect) who frequently ties the knot for romantic travelers. Linda, also born and raised in New Mexico, operates the inn's art gallery.

The Lundeens' establishment is itself a marriage of sorts. Two one-hundred-year-old adobes were creatively joined by Jerry to create Inn of the Arts, and the patio that once separated them became the inn's soaring living room. This room, called the Merienda, also functions occasionally as a classroom when area artists, craftspeople, actors, and writers conduct seminars and lectures.

ROOMS FOR ROMANCE

The Ken Barrick and Tony Hillerman Rooms (low $100 range) are adjacent freestanding century-old casitas that are favorites among couples seeking romantic and private retreats. Barrick has a full kitchen, a fireplace, a queen-sized bed, and a private courtyard patio. The Hillerman Room holds a fireplace that was designed by Jerry, in addition to a full kitchen.

In the main building, the Olaf Weighorst Room (low $100 range) features two queen-sized beds and a woodburning stove. In the bathroom, a red clawfoot tub with a shower extension is draped in netting.

The guest room pictured here is the Maria Martinez Room (under $100), one of the Southwest's romantic bargains. This sunny room has a fireplace and dark hardwood floors, and it's lit from south- and west-facing windows. It overlooks the garden and an adobe gazebo. The bathroom has *saltillo* tiles and a tub-and-shower combination.

Georgia O'Keeffe (under $100) is a popular second-floor room with a balcony and an unusual antique freestanding mantel into which the bed has been placed. Artist R. C. Gorman's namesake room has a private entrance, a kiva fireplace, and a partial viga ceiling, as well as a cozy built-in seating nook.

CASAS DE SUEÑOS
310 Rio Grande Boulevard SW
Albuquerque, NM 87104
Telephone: (505) 247-4560;
toll-free: (800) 665-7002
www.casasdesuenos.com

THE FACTS
Seventeen rooms, each with private bath; five with fire-places. Complimentary full breakfast served at tables for two. Disabled access. Two-night minimum stay required during weekends; three-night minimum during holiday periods. Moderate.

GETTING THERE
From Interstate 25 in Albuquerque, take Lomas Boulevard exit and drive west. Follow through downtown for approximately three miles. Turn left of Rio Grande Boulevard and follow to inn on left.

CASAS DE SUEÑOS

The folks at Casas de Sueños recall with pride the story of a couple who, after exchanging wedding vows on the inn's enchanting grounds, bid their families and friends goodbye and departed under the traditional shower of rice. Purportedly bound for some distant honeymoon destination, the cunning couple instead drove around the block and, unbeknownst to the wedding guests, quietly snuggled into the inn's honeymoon suite.

After touring the cozy rooms and the lush gardens of Casas de Sueños, we understood why the inn has become not only a favorite wedding site but a choice honeymoon destination.

Once an artists' compound, Casas de Sueños is by no means a predictable or typical bed-and-breakfast inn. The guest rooms, which used to be private residences, are delightfully diverse, and some of the architecture—the snail-shaped building that greets arriving guests, for example—is a bit quirky. Spring and summer visitors will find the interior courtyard and gardens in colorful bloom. Old Town is only three blocks away.

ROOMS FOR ROMANCE

Secret Garden (high $100 range) is considered the inn's honeymoon destination. It has a spacious bedroom and a sitting room with a love seat, and there's a private hot tub and a patio.

You walk under a grape arbor to enter Elliot Porter's Cottage (mid $100 range), one of our favorites. Located at the center of the gardens, this freestanding accommodation has a drawing room with a love seat, a kitchen, and a small bathroom with an unusual marble soaking tub. French doors lead from the bedroom to a private courtyard with a hot tub.

A separate room with a soft-sided six-foot spa is the main attraction of the Sueños Room (upper $100 range), which faces a grassy courtyard. The room has a king-sized bed, and the bathroom is equipped with a tub-and-shower combination.

A garden waterfall in your private courtyard sends romantically soothing sounds through La Cascada (low $100 range), a two-room unit with a queen-sized bed and a separate sitting room.

Although the Taos and Zuni Rooms occupy what in our opinion is a less desirable spot just outside the main compound, both are boldly decorated with colorful murals hand-painted by famed regional artist Amado Peña.

THE FACTS

Ten rooms, each with private bath. Complimentary full breakfast served at tables for four or more. Complimentary afternoon refreshments. No disabled access. No minimum-stay requirement. Moderate.

GETTING THERE

From Interstate 25 in Albuquerque, take Lomas Boulevard exit and drive west. Follow through downtown for approximately three miles and turn right on San Felipe. Inn is on right.

BOTTGER MANSION OF OLD TOWN ALBUQUERQUE

Albuquerque-bound couples with an eye toward experiencing the city's historic Old Town needn't look outside the district for a romantic weekend hideaway. The historic Bottger Mansion, which today offers ten elegant rooms and a delightful, shady yard, is wonderfully restored, right down to the high pressed-tin ceilings in some of the guest rooms. Individual heating and cooling units with remote controls are among the modern-day niceties that have been thoughtfully added.

Proprietors Steve and Kathy Hiatt, locals who both attended the University of New Mexico before careers and travels took them to other parts of the country, returned to Albuquerque to nurture this charming, well-tended establishment and to share their insights and suggestions with appreciative guests.

ROOMS FOR ROMANCE

The Stephanie Lynn Room, known as the inn's bridal suite, features a handsome queen-sized mahogany four-poster bed draped with a fishnet of pearl and fringe. A brass chandelier in the bathroom provides romantic lighting for a clawfoot tub. High season in Albuquerque runs from June through October, and the tariff during this period is in the upper $100 range.

Another romantic choice is the Rebecca Lee Room (upper $100 range), a large corner site furnished with a king-sized bed. A former sunporch has been converted into a light-filled bathroom with a spa tub.

Located just off the front entry, the Carole Rose (mid $100 range) is a two-room suite with a king-sized bed and a sunroom-turned-sitting-room. Guests in the Natalie Rose Room (low to mid $100 range) can open their windows and glimpse the white steeples of historic San Felipe de Neri Church in Old Town. This room has a queen-sized four-poster bed and a bathroom with a shower.

BOTTGER MANSION OF OLD TOWN
110 San Felipe NW
Albuquerque, NM 87104
Telephone: (505) 243-3639;
toll-free: (800) 758-3639
www.bottger.com

61

THE GALISTEO INN

9 La Vega Road
HC 75, P.O. Box 4
Galisteo, NM 87540
Telephone: (866) 404-8200
www.galisteoinn.com

THE FACTS

Twelve rooms, ten with private baths; four with woodburn-
ing fireplaces. Complimentary buffet breakfast served in
dining room. Swimming pool, hot tub, sauna, and horseback
riding. Restaurant with à la carte menu. Disabled access.
Two-night minimum stay required during high-season
weekends; three-night minimum during holiday periods.
Moderate to expensive.

GETTING THERE

From Santa Fe, follow Interstate 25 north and exit at
Highway 285. Drive south to Lamy and turn south on
Highway 41. Follow to Galisteo. At Nuestra Señora de los
Remidos Church, turn left and follow Via la Puente for
a tenth of a mile. Turn left on La Vega Road and follow
two-tenths of a mile to inn's driveway on right. Galisteo
is twenty-three miles from Santa Fe.

THE GALISTEO INN

The distance between the crumbling old adobes of Galisteo village and the sumptuous Galisteo Inn is less than one mile, but we felt as though we had traveled back a few hundred years in a time machine.

Actually, the contrast turned out to be somewhat less significant than our first impression indicated. The inn, we were told, was created from a hacienda that was built in the mid-1700s, making the Galisteo Inn the oldest of our fifty featured destinations.

Although there are some reminders of days gone by, like the old jail that stands on the property, don't expect a drafty room and earthen floors. The years, not to mention the innkeepers, have been kind to the historic structure, which has been completely refurbished and updated over time.

The inn is accessed via a tree-shaded gravel road that runs from the hamlet of Galisteo past comfortable Southwestern-style family homes. Pasture and lawn surround the rambling single-story inn, which is shaded by towering cottonwood trees.

Guests have access to a beautiful swimming pool and a hot tub, but a sixty-three-hundred-foot elevation ensures a comfortable summer environment. There's also an indoor sauna.

There are no restaurants in the area, so most guests take advantage of the inn's à la carte dinner menu. Mountain bikes are available to guests at no extra charge.

ROOMS FOR ROMANCE

The most expensive room is Tack Suite (around $200), a separate and spacious cottage with a king-sized bed and a kiva fireplace; it sits at the rear of the property facing a walled courtyard and the swimming pool. The tiled bathroom has double sinks.

The Santa Fe Suite (around $200), the hacienda's original master bedroom, is equipped with a king-sized bed and a fireplace. This corner room, which overlooks the front pasture with its sheep and horses, has a handsome viga ceiling and a bathroom with a double-headed shower.

Tano (mid $100 range), reached from the inn's beautiful main hallway with its viga ceiling and hardwood floors, has a fireplace and a queen-sized bed. Tano also faces the pasture.

Located in a separate cottage, the Galisteo Suite (around $200) is a sunny and bright two-bedroom suite with original photography, and picture windows that overlook the pasture. The room is equipped with a king-sized bed and a private patio. The Young Guns and La Cama rooms have shared bathrooms.

THE FACTS

One hundred eleven rooms and suites, each with private bath; many with fireplaces. Swimming pool, spa, saunas, fitness room, tennis courts, and horseback riding. Restaurant. Disabled access. Smoking allowed. No minimum stay requirement. Deluxe.

GETTING THERE

From Albuquerque, drive north on Interstate 25 and take St. Francis Drive (exit 282). Proceed north for four and a half miles and turn right on Paseo de Peralta (second intersection of Paseo de Peralta). At the fourth stoplight, turn left on Washington Avenue/Bishop's Lodge Road. Follow for three and a half miles to lodge entrance.

THE BISHOP'S LODGE RESORT AND SPA
Bishop's Lodge Road
Santa Fe, NM 87501
Telephone: (505) 983-6377;
toll-free: (800) 419-0492
www.bishopslodge.com

Santa Fe visitors who'd like to put a little distance between themselves and the busy downtown area at the end of the day need only venture three miles up Bishop's Lodge Road, where this venerable resort has been offering respite since the 1920s.

The thousand-acre resort consists of eleven separate adobe-style "lodges" that dot gentle hillsides covered with native juniper and piñon as well as fruit trees. One of the most enchanting spots on the property is a romantic little adobe chapel reached by a footpath. Many a marriage has been made here.

Guests have access to a heated pool, a large indoor spa, an exercise room, and men's and women's saunas. There's an extra charge for tennis, skeet shooting, and horseback riding. The resort offers a free daily shuttle service to and from downtown Santa Fe.

Rates here are at their peak from July through Labor Day, when the resort bustles with families enjoying summer vacations above the desert heat. Tariffs are considerably less in the fall, winter, and spring, when you're more apt to see couples strolling the quiet grounds. For example, the deluxe rooms that receive our highest recommendation command well over $300 during the summer. The same rooms are offered in the low $200 range at certain other times of the year.

Since our first visit, the lodge has opened the ShaNah Spa, with a menu of more than two dozen decadent services.

ROOMS FOR ROMANCE

Although the resort's rooms are all comfortable, some of the older units we toured were fairly plain; a few were a bit dated. We were most consistently impressed with the Chamisa Lodge, and we recommend the rooms here for romantic getaways.

This two-story pueblo-style building is among the more recent additions to the lodge, and it holds more than a dozen spacious and contemporary-style rooms. The setting among trees is a plus.

Among the accommodations here is room 204, which overlooks an adjacent creek and trees. The room is appointed with a couch, a Craftsman-style chair, a corner gas kiva fireplace, and a king-sized bed, placed at an angle in a corner. The large tiled bath holds two sinks, a shower stall, and a deep soaking tub that just might hold both of you.

THE FACTS

Twelve rooms and suites, each with private bath. Complimentary full breakfast served at small tables. Disabled access. Two-night minimum stay required. Moderate to expensive.

GETTING THERE

From Interstate 25, exit at Old Pecos Trail and drive north into Santa Fe. Turn left on Paseo de Peralta, then left on Don Gaspar Avenue. The compound is one and a half blocks on left. To reach the office, follow Don Gaspar Avenue to corner, turn left on Booth Street and left at alley. Park behind adobe wall and walk through gate to office.

THE DON GASPAR INN

623 Don Gaspar Avenue
Santa Fe, NM 87501
Telephone: (505) 986-8664;
toll-free: (888) 986-8664
www.dongaspar.com

THE DON GASPAR INN

During a visit to the impressive Blue Lake Ranch in southwestern Colorado (see separate listing), we learned that innkeepers David and Shirley Alford also own the Don Gaspar Inn in New Mexico. Impressed by what the couple had created in Colorado, we decided to take a look at the Santa Fe property. You'll be glad we did.

Set within an adobe-walled garden courtyard, the compound is located in the Don Gaspar Historic District, just a short distance from the state capitol and a mile or so from the downtown plaza.

ROOMS FOR ROMANCE

The Courtyard Casita (low $200 range), a private apartment-sized suite with Mexican *saltillo* tile floors, boasts glorious floor-to-ceiling French windows in the living room that offer views of the garden fountain. French doors open onto a private patio, and there's a gas fireplace and a kitchen as well. The living room furniture, perfect for siestas, is overscaled and overstuffed. The bedroom contains a king-sized bed, and the bathroom is equipped with a spa tub for two.

The Fountain Casita (around $200) also has *saltillo* tile floors, a gas fireplace, and a queen-sized bed. The view of the fountain through the living room's French doors is a romantic plus.

A separate adobe building houses the Southwest, Aspen, and Colorado suites. Southwest (around $200) has a large adobe fireplace and a dining table for two in the living room. The bedroom holds a king-sized bed.

In Colorado (mid $100 range), French doors open onto a patio. This suite has a spacious bedroom with a queen-sized bed and a sitting area that overlooks the garden. There's also a fireplace, and a kitchenette occupies a hallway alcove.

Aspen (high $100 range) is a one-bedroom suite with a king-sized bed, a separate living room, a fireplace, a window seat, and nice garden views through aspen trees.

There's also a three-bedroom, two-bathroom home that's rented as one unit to families or to couples traveling together.

THE FACTS

Fifty-six rooms, each with private bath and gas fireplace. Fitness room. Restaurant. Disabled access. Four-night minimum stay required during peak season and holiday periods. Deluxe.

GETTING THERE

From Albuquerque, drive north on Interstate 25; exit at St. Francis Drive/Highway 285 and follow north to second Paseo de Peralta exit. Turn right and follow into downtown Santa Fe. Turn right on Washington Avenue and follow to inn on left.

INN OF THE ANASAZI

Those who have spent any time in the Southwest are aware of the tendency among some interior designers to overdose on generic or clichéd regional décor, from cactus lamps to log furnishings.

At Inn of the Anasazi (*anasazi* is Navajo for "the ancient ones") the perfect balance has been struck. You won't be overwhelmed by Southwestern kitsch, but neither will there be any doubt about where you are.

Understated and elegant, the inn isn't fussy, yet the feeling is rich, textured, and inviting. It also enjoys a perfect location for shoppers and downtown explorers, just steps from the historic plaza. Without a doubt, this is *the* place to stay in Santa Fe. It's also one of the priciest of our recommended romantic retreats.

ROOMS FOR ROMANCE

The accommodations consist of deluxe rooms (high $400 range), superior king rooms (high $300 range), and somewhat small standard rooms with king-sized beds (around $300). From November through March, rates are lower.

For a memorable romantic getaway, we recommend a select superior room (low $400 range), which offers a sitting srea with a sofa. Some have tree-shaded balconies. Suites are even more comfortable.

All of the inn's guest rooms are subtly yet comfortably styled. The walls are hand-plastered, the pine floors are covered with handsome rugs, and the ceilings, themselves works of art, boast traditional vigas inlaid with patterned *latillas*. Light is provided by attractive lamps, some fashioned from twisted wrought iron. Four-posted iron beds and gas-lit kiva-style fireplaces complement the romantic ambience.

Amenities here include twice-daily maid service. The inn also has an exercise room.

The Anasazi Restaurant features award-winning contemporary Southwestern cuisine.

INN OF THE ANASAZI
113 Washington Avenue
Santa Fe, NM 87501
Telephone: (505) 988-3030;
toll-free: (800) 688-8100
www.innoftheanasazi.com

GRANT CORNER INN
122 Grant Avenue
Santa Fe, NM 87501
Telephone: (505) 983-6678;
toll-free: (800) 964-9003
www.grantcornerinn.com

THE FACTS

*Twelve rooms, ten with private baths. Complimentary full
breakfast served at tables for two and four in dining room,
on deck, or in your room. Restaurant. Disabled access.
Three-night minimum stay required during holiday periods.
Moderate to expensive.*

GETTING THERE

*From Albuquerque, drive north on Interstate 25 and exit
at St. Francis Drive/Highway 285; it's approximately
four miles into Santa Fe. Turn right on Alameda, left on
Guadalupe, and right on Johnson. Inn is on corner of Grant
and Johnson Avenues.*

GRANT CORNER INN

Displaying a stunning gabled façade that turns the heads of passing motorists and slows the strolls of all but the most determined pedestrians, Grant Corner Inn is one of Santa Fe's best-known inns, famous not only for its beds but for its breakfasts as well. An afterthought at so many inns, the morning meal is one of the main attractions here. In fact, weekend brunch, served on white wrought-iron tables on the columned and covered front porch, is popular with city residents and overnight guests alike.

Located two blocks from Santa Fe's famous plaza, Grant Corner Inn is operated by longtime innkeeper Louise Stewart. Louise, whose father founded the Camelback Inn in Scottsdale, is also an accomplished interior designer.

The proprietress also operates the Grant Corner Inn Hacienda, a Southwestern-style condo with two guest rooms, each offered in the low $100 range. The Hacienda is located about five blocks from the inn.

ROOMS FOR ROMANCE

Of the inn's dozen accommodations, our favorites for a romantic getaway are rooms 3, 4, 7, 8, and 10. Arguably the nicest accommodation, room 4 (mid $200 range) is a regal-looking room with a richly dressed king-sized partially canopied bed flanked by two windows with matching draperies. The bathroom has a spa tub.

Decorated in soft red tones, room 8 (mid $200 range) on the second floor holds a king-sized brass-and-iron bed, a reproduction Austrian ceramic stove, and an antique love seat. The bathroom has a shower stall. Guests here share the balcony with room 7, located next door.

Room 7 (mid $200 range) is the only accommodation featuring Southwestern décor. The center-piece is a grand king-sized draped pencil-post bed made of pine. Native American rugs cover the floor, and the bathroom has a tiled tub-and-shower combination.

Located high on the third floor under the eaves, the very private room 10 (low to high $100 range) has mauve-colored walls, a queen-sized bed, and a cozy sitting area with a love seat.

Room 3 (around $200) occupies a rear corner on the second floor and is appointed with a queen-sized draped iron four-poster bed and an in-room antique sink. The tiled bathroom has a tiled tub-and-shower combination.

The bathroom for room 11 is across the hall.

ALEXANDER'S INN

529 East Palace Avenue
Santa Fe, NM 87501
Telephone: (505) 986-1431;
toll-free: (888) 321-5123
www.alexanders-inn.com

THE FACTS

*Ten rooms, eight with private baths. Complimentary full
breakfast served at communal table or smaller tables,
or delivered to your room. Complimentary refreshments.
Communal spa. Health club privileges. Free bike rental.
No disabled access. Behaved pets welcome. Two-night
minimum stay required during weekends; three-night
minimum during holiday periods. Moderate to expensive.*

GETTING THERE

*From Albuquerque, drive north on Interstate 25 and exit at
St. Francis Drive. Turn right on Cerrillos and right on Paseo
de Peralta. Follow as it curves. Turn right on Palace Avenue
to inn on left.*

ALEXANDER'S INN

Innkeeper Carolyn Lee is a native Midwestern girl and diplomat's daughter who's come a long way since her childhood in a small Iowa town. After dancing ballet professionally, she attended college at Tufts, spent a few years working on Wall Street, and even lived in Paris for a time.

Life took yet another turn in 1988 when Carolyn headed west, bought a charming home five blocks from Santa Fe's historic plaza, and set about converting it into an inn. Several years and three children later, Carolyn's inn, named lovingly after her son, has emerged as a favored destination among romantics in-the-know.

One of the neighborhood's oldest homes, the Craftsman-style inn with dormer windows has been reverently restored and comfortably appointed. Carolyn's touch is also evident in the outside gardens, profuse with colorful blooms of the season. There's also a comfortable veranda and a backyard spa for guests' use. Canyon Road art galleries are just three blocks away.

ROOMS FOR ROMANCE

The Lilac Room (around $200) is a spacious and colorful downstairs corner room with stained-glass windows, a large brick fireplace, an antique love seat, and a handsome king-sized four-poster bed. The bathroom has a clawfoot tub. This room also comes with a coveted on-site parking space. Other guests park down the street.

The Casita (around $200), a two-level hideaway accessed through a rear parking area, features a downstairs sitting area with two comfortable leather chairs and a kiva fireplace. Upstairs is a king-sized bed. The bathroom has a tub-and-shower combination.

Located a few steps from the main house, the Cottage (low $200 range) is a virtual home away from home. The lower level features a nice living room with a couch and a kiva fireplace, a cozy dining area, and a full kitchen with colorful tile. The bathroom has a spa tub for two. A spiral stairway leads to a sunny loft bedroom under the eaves.

The Peony and Wildflower Rooms share a bathroom; the bathroom for the lovely Lavender Room is a step or two across the hall. Carolyn's properties also include a couple of nearby homes available for overnight or longer stays. The inn is dog-friendly.

THE FACTS

One hundred fifty-seven rooms, each with private bath; many with fireplaces. Restaurant and lounge. Swimming pool and communal spa. Fitness center. Day spa. Disabled access. Multinight stay required during certain time periods; call for details. Expensive to deluxe.

GETTING THERE

From Albuquerque, drive north on Interstate 25 and exit at St. Francis Drive. Drive north to Paseo de Peralta and turn right. Turn right on Palace Avenue. Resort is on corner on right.

LA POSADA DE SANTA FE
330 East Palace Avenue
Santa Fe, NM 87501
Telephone: (505) 986-0000;
toll-free: (866) 331-ROCK
www.rockresorts.com

LA POSADA DE SANTA FE

We have the venerable *Architectural Digest* magazine to thank for bringing our attention to this romantic Santa Fe destination. Although in earlier days the property functioned as an arts colony and later as a funky motor lodge, recently the collection of adobe-style casitas was transformed into an impressive oasis just two blocks from Santa Fe's Plaza. The "regeneration" of the resort included a stylish makeover, the replacement of roadways with winding footpaths, the creation of new accommodations, and the addition of a full-service day spa.

Resorts of this size (La Posada has over 150 rooms) typically don't find their way into the pages of *Weekends for Two*, but we made an exception for this delightful destination, which is anything but cookie-cutter in its layout or design.

The rambling six-acre resort is dotted with a number of attractive buildings, each housing a handful of rooms and suites. They're interconnected by paths that wind throughout the property past fountains, terraces, sculpture, and lawns. Avanyu, a full-service day spa, sits at the center of the resort. Nearby is the historic Staab House, a stately Victorian mansion that now houses Las Posada's lounge as well as a handful of comfortable guest rooms. The Del Fuego restaurant on the property offers more romantic dining.

ROOMS FOR ROMANCE

Room décor might best be described as casual Spanish colonial. The resort offers multiple room-level categories. Deluxe Rooms (upper $200 range) have king- or queen-sized beds and a fireplace and/or a private patio. Classic Junior Suites (around $400) are oversized guest rooms with a sitting area and a queen-sized or king-sized bed. Deluxe Junior Suites (mid $400 range) have fireplaces and/or patios. The junior suites range in size from four hundred to six hundred square feet.

La Posada also offers a collection of "Gallery Suites," each decorated with original works by respected artists. Media include photography, glass, metal sculpture, stone, and canvas.

We enjoyed room 237, an impressive second-floor suite overlooking the pool. This and certain other suites are lavished with tens of thousands of dollars worth of original regional art.

WATER STREET INN

427 West Water Street
Santa Fe, NM 87501
Telephone: (505) 984-1193;
toll-free: (800) 646-6752
www.waterstreetinn.com

THE FACTS

Twelve rooms, each with private bath; eight with fireplaces. Complimentary continental breakfast served at communal table or delivered to your room. Complimentary evening refreshments. Communal spa. Disabled access. Three-night minimum stay required during holiday periods. Moderate to expensive.

GETTING THERE

From Albuquerque, drive north on Interstate 25 and exit at St. Francis Drive. Turn right on Cerrillos Road, left on Guadalupe, and left on West Water. Drive a half block to inn on right.

WATER STREET INN

As one of America's perennial top-ten favorite domestic vacation destinations, Santa Fe merits more attention than any city we've featured in our multiple *Weekends for Two* volumes. One of our newest finds is this discreet pueblo-style inn with a central location and competitive rates that have earned raves from guests.

Don't expect expanses of lawns or inspirational views, the parking lot is literally outside your door. Although it may lack an idyllic setting, the Water Street Inn's location (only a short walk from the Plaza) is a decided plus.

ROOMS FOR ROMANCE

Decorated with a playful and colorful mix of cowboy camp, playful Latin, and more traditional Southwest, the inn boasts more than a few rooms that are conducive to romance. Among the unique touches are the additional daybeds—or *bancos*—found in a few of the rooms. Couples traveling with a child will find one use for these, while friendly twosomes will likely find another way to enjoy them.

Among our favorite lodgings is the Tesuque Suite (low $200 range), the inn's largest accommodation, with a pretty queen-sized pediment-style bed and two additional beds. This two-room affair has two corner fireplaces and a private patio. We also like the Atalya, which offers a small private patio off of a miniature sunroom.

Room 7 (low $200 range) is a second-floor hideaway accessed by a private spiral stairway. This room has a woodburning stove, a beamed ceiling, a private deck, built-in bookcases, and a spa tub.

In the upper $100 range is room 3, furnished with a queen-sized log-and-iron bed, a love seat, and an antique gas stove. In the same price range is room 2, which has a king-sized antique pine bed and a raised fireplace.

THE FACTS

Eight rooms, each with private bath, patio, and private entrance; seven with fireplaces. Complimentary expanded continental breakfast served at tables for two or more or delivered to your room. No disabled access. Two-night minimum stay required if Saturday-night stay is desired; three- to four-night minimum during holidays. Moderate to expensive.

GETTING THERE

From Albuquerque, drive north on Interstate 25 and exit at St. Francis Drive. Turn right on Cerrillos Road, right on Paseo de Peralta, and left on Galisteo. Inn is on left.

EL FAROLITO BED-AND-BREAKFAST INN
514 Galisteo Street
Santa Fe, NM 87501
Telephone: (505) 988-1631;
toll-free: (888) 634-8782
www.farolito.com

EL FAROLITO BED-AND-BREAKFAST INN

Outside Santa Fe, those distinctively Southwestern candles-in-a-paper-bag are called *luminarias*. In Santa Fe, they're referred to as *farolitos*. Maybe that's one of the reasons why locals refer to their town as the "City Different."

Distinctively romantic is how we'd describe El Farolito, which differentiates itself from other inns by providing such thoughtful features as spacious accommodations, kiva fireplaces, and private patios. Some of El Farolito's casitas also offer couches or pairs of comfy chairs that can be slid together before a flickering fire.

The inn, whose sister property is the Four Kachinas Inn (see separate listing), consists of seven rooms in four Santa Fe–style adobe buildings, as well as one suite. All accommodations have cable televisions and air conditioning, as well as private entries and patios or courtyard areas. The casitas all have kiva fireplaces, and bathrooms feature hand-painted tiles. Original Southwestern art, weavings, and folk art contribute to the ambience. Bathrooms are purely functional.

Breakfast is served at tables for two or more in a delightful room with a traditional Southwestern exposed-beam ceiling and a large fireplace.

ROOMS FOR ROMANCE

The dark-tile-floored room 7, called Casita San Pasqual (around $200), has a couch placed next to a cozy kiva fireplace. The queen-sized bed is placed at an angle facing the fireplace and the French doors to a common patio.

One of the most attractive accommodations is room 3, the Acequia Madre (around $200), which has an exposed-beam ceiling, a brick floor, a king-sized wooden sleigh-style bed, a raised kiva fire-place with a brick hearth, and a cozy corner sitting area with two chairs.

Room 8, the Santa Fe Suite (low $200 range), has a small living room with a sofa bed but, alas, no fireplace. This room faces a street with a fair amount of traffic. Casita Peralta is equipped with two double beds. At the time of our travels, casitas 5 and 6, both with queen-sized beds, were offered for slightly less than $200.

FOUR KACHINAS INN

512 Webber Street
Santa Fe, NM 87501
Telephone: (505) 982-2550;
toll-free: (800) 397-2564
www.fourkachinas.com

THE FACTS

Five rooms, each with private bath and private entry. Complimentary extended continental breakfast served at tables for two, outdoors, or delivered to your room. Complimentary refreshments. Communal spa. Limited disabled access. Two-night minimum stay if Saturday-night stay is desired; three- to four-night minimum stay during holiday periods. Moderate.

GETTING THERE

From Albuquerque, drive north on Interstate 25 and exit at St. Francis Drive. Follow north and turn right on Cerrillos Road. Turn right on Paseo de Peralta. Follow for three blocks and turn right on Webber Street (directly south of the state capitol). Inn is second property on right.

In this destination city, where nightly tariffs for romantic accommodations are pushing stratospheric levels, we found Four Kachinas to be a relative bargain. Offering rates that are half of those charged at some other Santa Fe properties, this quaint, centrally located inn is a great value for traveling romantics on a budget.

Situated just around the corner from New Mexico's state capitol in a historic neighborhood, Four Kachinas Inn was created during the 1990s in the northern New Mexico Territorial style, characterized by its red pitched-tin roof. Guests may access the city's popular plaza on foot via the Old Santa Fe Trail.

ROOMS FOR ROMANCE

Our top guest room picks are the four in the newer building built around a courtyard. Arguably the most romantic is room 4, the Chimayó Room (around $200), a spacious retreat with a tiled floor, a vaulted ceiling, sunny window seating, a sofa bed, an armoire, and a king-sized bed.

Another good romantic choice is room 1, Kachina (high $100 range). This privately situated natural-toned hideaway has a high ceiling, handsome Native American weavings, kachina dolls, a queen-sized bed, and a sofa bed.

Room 2, the Zia Room (high $100 range) has a cathedral ceiling, Southwestern art, and a king-sized bed, while the Mexican-themed San Miguel Room (high $100 range) is furnished with dual queen-sized wrought-iron beds and leather chairs.

Room 5 (mid $100 range), is located in an adjacent century-old home built by Carlo Digneo, an Italian stonemason who worked on Santa Fe Cathedral.

Rooms 1,2, and 3 have small private patios.

The Four Kachinas Inn and El Farolito are under the same hospitable ownership.

THE FACTS

Twenty-two rooms, each with private bath; most with fireplaces and kitchen facilities. Complimentary full breakfast. Complimentary afternoon and evening refreshments. Twice-daily housekeeping. Disabled access. Pets welcome. Deluxe.

GETTING THERE

From Albuquerque, drive north on Interstate 25 and exit at St. Francis Drive. Follow for approximately four miles. Turn right on Alameda and drive approximately one mile. Turn right on Don Gaspar and turn left on East DeVargas. Inn's office is on right just past Santa Fe Playhouse.

THE INN OF THE FIVE GRACES
150 East DeVargas Street
Santa Fe, NM 87501
Telephone: (505) 992-0957
www.fivegraces.com

THE INN OF THE FIVE GRACES

For travelers wanting to ensure a memorable romantic experience by taking no chances in booking suitable accommodations, we recommend a stay at The Inn of the Five Graces, quite possibly the region's most enchanting destination.

A tasteful and graceful melding of Asian and Old West styles, the inn drew its inspiration from previous owners, who filled the former apartment compound with their Oriental rug and antiques collection. The Garret Hotel Group, which also operates the famous Pointe Resort in upstate New York, took over in 2002, changing the name while wisely preserving the inn's uniquely rich and sensual atmosphere. *Architectural Digest* magazine was sufficiently impressed to feature the inn in its pages.

ROOMS FOR ROMANCE

Guest rooms are spread among multiple charming buildings facing a narrow lane in the shadow of the state capitol. The rooms, most of which have kitchens and average over four hundred square feet in size, face well-tended courtyards with gardens and places to relax. The custom-made feather beds are luxuriously fitted with Belgian linens and down comforters.

Room 13 (upper $300 range), described as a Junior Suite, has a private ivy-covered patio, a stone kiva fireplace, and a queen-sized canopy bed. The bathroom has a spa tub in a colorful tiled surround.

There are a number of full suites (around $400) with separate living rooms. Suites 16 and 17 are popular upstairs retreats and are furnished with queen-sized beds and clawfoot-tub-and-shower combinations. Suite 16 has a small courtyard view deck. Most furnishings are hand-carved and covered in bright imported fabrics. The kitchens are spacious and boast slate floors and colorful tile work.

We still reminisce about the night we spent in room 19, a rambling, exotic suite with intricately carved doors and cabinets, colorful rugs, and a hand-painted tin ceiling. In the bathroom, a spa tub for two sits in a colorful mosaic surround of tile and ceramic pieces.

THE FACTS

*Sixty-nine rooms, each with private bath. Complimentary
extensive continental breakfast buffet taken at tables
for two or four or delivered to your room at extra charge.
Complimentary afternoon wine and cheese reception.
Lounge. Communal spas. Fitness facility. Disabled access.
Two-night minimum stay required during certain periods.
Expensive to deluxe.*

GETTING THERE

*From Interstate 25, exit at Old Pecos Trail north and follow
as road bears right. Turn right on Paseo de Peralta and
right on East Alameda. Inn is on right.*

INN ON THE ALAMEDA

Inn on the Alameda first caught our eye in a prominent travel magazine's listing of the world's best hotels, included alongside such more famous names as Four Seasons and Ritz-Carlton. After a personal visit, the sixty-nine-room, pueblo-style inn likewise earned a spot on our list of the Southwest's most romantic destinations.

From the street, it's the inn's signature bell tower that distinguishes the property. Inside, it is the attentive customer orientation and luxurious atmosphere that keep guests coming back. Boasting a comparatively high staff-to-guest ratio, the inn prides itself on service. Employees are concierge-trained and eager to please, available and ready with informed advice on the community and region.

The inn also goes above and beyond on cuisine despite the lack of a restaurant. In the morning, guests are treated to a lavish continental breakfast buffet, and afternoons are highlighted by complimentary wine and cheese. There's also a wine and cocktail lounge whose specialty is a tasty Turquoise Magarita.

Guests also have Santa Fe at their feet. The art galleries of Canyon Road are just down the street, and Santa Fe Plaza is only three blocks away.

ROOMS FOR ROMANCE

While the inn's self-described traditional rooms with king-sized beds (mid $200 range) are comfortable and well-appointed, couples intent on a romantic getaway should consider a deluxe room (around $300) or a suite (high $300 range).

Deluxe rooms are spacious and feature traditional-style furnishings, local art, and nice bathrooms with tile and wrought-iron touches. These rooms also come with a private balcony or patio, and feature either a kiva fireplace or a lounging sofa.

Suites are even larger and more luxurious. Most have separate living rooms and bedrooms along with hardwood floors, kiva fireplaces, and Persian rugs. Pets are welcome.

INN ON THE ALAMEDA
303 East Alameda
Santa Fe, NM 87501
Telephone: (505) 984-2121;
toll-free: (800) 289-2122
www.innonthealameda.com

THE FACTS

Twenty rooms, each with private bath and woodburning fireplace. Complimentary continental breakfast served at tables for two or taken to your room. Complimentary refreshments served in the afternoon. Indoor communal hot tub. Limited disabled access. No minimum stay requirement. Moderate.

GETTING THERE

From Interstate 25, exit at Old Pecos Trail north and follow into Santa Fe. Turn left on Paseo de Peralta and turn right on Manhattan Street. Inn is on left at corner of Manhattan and Galisteo.

PUEBLO BONITO

Traveling couples looking for a romantic Southwest experience without busting their budgets will appreciate this pleasant inn just around the corner from the New Mexico state capitol. At the time of our most recent travels, cozy rooms with woodburning corner kivas, traditional viga ceilings, and private baths were available at high-season rates of less than $150, a relative bargain in this popular destination city. During winter months, rates below $100 are a steal.

Formerly a private estate dating from the early 1900s, Pueblo Bonito now consists of twenty guest rooms, all of which are equipped with fireplaces. Although some of the furnishings and décor were looking a bit tired at last glance, the rooms are still a good comparative value, especially given that breakfast is included in the room rate. Bathrooms are small but functional.

Eleven rooms and a single suite are contained within a two-story building, while several suites are strung together along the rear of the property. Brick paths wind through lush courtyards and gardens, and adobe archways open onto the city streets.

A continental breakfast buffet is served either in the communal dining room or outdoors on the patio. Margaritas, wine, cheese, and crackers are offered each afternoon.

PUEBLO BONITO
138 West Manhattan Avenue
Santa Fe, NM 87501
Telephone: (505) 984-8001;
toll-free: (800) 461-4599
www.pueblobonitoinn.com

ROOMS FOR ROMANCE

According to the folks at Pueblo Bonito, Comanche (mid $100 range) is "everybody's favorite." This tight and cozy hideaway, the only suite contained in the two-story building, has a seperate bedroom with a king-sized bed, kiva fireplace, and maple floors. There's a queen-sized futon in the sitting room.

The other suites (mid $100 range) are good romantic choices as well. Each has a separate sitting room with a futon, a kiva fireplace, and a kitchen.

RANCHO DE SAN JUAN
Highway 285 at Mile 340
P.O. Box 4140
Espanola, NM 87532
Telephone: (505) 753-6818;
toll-free: (800) 726-7121
www.ranchodesanjuan.com

THE FACTS

Seventeen rooms, each with private bath, fireplace, and CD player. Restaurant serves breakfast and fixed-price dinners. Lounge. Massage treatments. Disabled access. Minimum stay required during major holiday periods. Expensive to deluxe.

GETTING THERE

The inn is approximately thirty-five miles northwest of Santa Fe. From Santa Fe, drive north on Highway 84/285 to Española. Turn left on Fairview Drive and turn right on Highway 84. Follow for six and a half miles to Highway 285. Turn right and follow for three and a half miles. Two large columns and a sign mark drive on right.

RANCHO DE SAN JUAN

Traveling romantics owe a great debt to David Heath and John Johnson, who drew from their dreams, vision, and skills to imagine, design, and craft this idyllic high-desert retreat.

Guests here are at once surrounded by the craggy pinnacles of the Jemez Mountains and cosseted in the luxury of seventeen wonderful guest rooms and a dining room furnished with Limoges china.

One of the most intriguing parts of the remote, romantic rancho was carved literally out of the desert. Sculptor Ra Paulette used hand tools to burrow into solid stone, fashioning an awe-inspiring natural shrine with intricate carvings and an egg-shaped meditation center. The Sandstone Shrine is a short walk from the main area and a must-see for traveling romantics. In fact, this spiritual place has been the site of a few weddings.

ROOMS FOR ROMANCE

Created a decade or so ago with only five rooms, the inn has grown in popularity and size. Today, there are seventeen rooms and suites, each possessing its own stylish personality. While rates here climb into the $400 range, we were pleasantly surprised to discover a handful of nice standard rooms offered during the time of our travels for around $200, give or take a few dollars. In this category, we were impressed with the San Juan Room (low $200 range), a spacious tiled retreat boasting great views, a king-sized bed, and a private patio.

The circular junior suite called Kiva (high $300 range) has an almost spiritual feel. Cushioned *banco*-style seating encircles the room whose centerpieces are a king-sized bed, a chenille sofa, and a kiva fireplace. The Italian-tiled bathroom is a romantic's dream, offering a large spa tub and a separate shower.

The main level of the ultra-romantic Anasazi Casita Suite (low $400 range) consists of a spacious living area with a Southwestern-style sofa and a raised fireplace. Three steps lead to a beautiful bedchamber with a king-sized draped bed. The bathroom boasts a view, a whirlpool tub for two, and a separate shower. None of the rooms have televisions, although all are equipped with computer data ports.

THE FACTS

Nine rooms, each with private bath, sitting area, and CD player; most with woodburning kiva fireplaces; five with tubs for two. Complimentary full breakfast served at tables for two. Complimentary afternoon refreshments. No disabled access. Smoking not permitted indoors. Two-night minimum stay required during weekends; four-night minimum during holiday periods. Moderate.

GETTING THERE

Inn is located approximately four miles south of Taos and a half mile south of the Historic Ranchos Plaza, just off the east side of Highway 68.

ADOBE PINES INN
Highway 68
Ranchos de Taos, NM 87557
Telephone: (505) 751-0947;
toll-free: (800) 723-8267
www.adobepines.com

In anticipation of reaching the historic downtown area, most Taos-bound couples heading north along Highway 68 are probably unaware that one of New Mexico's most romantic inns sits just off the road, less than ten minutes from town. This somewhat-hidden location only contributes to the allure of Adobe Pines Inn, among our most prized Southwestern discoveries.

Guests reach the vintage 1830s adobe home-turned-inn by crossing a footbridge over a creek. The structure is fronted by a grassy courtyard and a grand portal with a stone floor and a viga ceiling. Comfortable chairs are placed along its eighty-foot expanse.

David and Kay Ann Tyssee, new proprietors since our first visit, have been careful to preserve the inn's antique charm and authentic detailing. However, visitors will appreciate improvements like modern bathrooms.

ROOMS FOR ROMANCE

Adobe Pines Inn holds two of the Southwest's most romantic rooms: Puerta Rosa and Puerta Violeta. Puerta Rosa (high $100 range), which has a viga ceiling and a polished brick floor, is appointed with antiques and a corner kiva fireplace.

The queen-sized bed has a wrought-iron headboard. The most romantic feature, however, is five steps down from the bedroom, where a grand bathroom awaits. This slice of heaven, which comes complete with bubble bath and candles, has wide pine floors and a viga ceiling, its own kiva fireplace, a sitting area, tiled double sinks, a tiled soaking tub for two, a tiled shower stall, and a sauna for two.

Puerta Violeta (mid $100 range) is the inn's only second-floor guest room, and it offers a private roof deck. A queen-sized iron bed sits on a pine wood floor in front of a corner kiva fireplace. A couple of steps up from the bedroom is a beautiful tiled bath with an oval spa tub for two under a treetop window. There's also a separate shower stall. This room has a view of Taos Mountain.

Puerta Cobre and Puerta Roja (high $100 range) also have very romantic bathrooms with spa tubs for two and fireplaces.

Located off the main portal, Puerta Azul is the inn's smallest room, offered at the time of our visit for a bargain tariff of around $100. This intriguing hideaway, with a queen-sized bed and a kiva fireplace, exudes an almost spiritual ambience. Puerta Verde (around $100) has a small bathroom that's separated from the room by a half-wall.

CASA DE LAS CHIMENEAS
BED-AND-BREAKFAST INN

405 Cordoba Road
Taos, NM 87571
Telephone: (505) 758-4777;
toll-free: (877) 758-4777
www.visittaos.com

THE FACTS

Eight rooms, each with private bath, kiva fireplace, refrigerator with complimentary drinks, television, and videocassette player. Complimentary full breakfast served at a communal table, smaller tables, or in your room. Complimentary light buffet supper. Hot tub. Fitness room. Dry sauna. Spa treatments available. Guest laundry facilities. No disabled access. No minimum stay requirement. Expensive to deluxe.

GETTING THERE

From Highway 68 just south of Taos's historic downtown center, turn east on Los Pandos Road. Drive one block to Cordoba Road (four-way stop) and turn right. Inn is on left.

CASA DE LAS CHIMENEAS BED-AND-BREAKFAST INN

Thumb through the pages of this book and you'll notice that we tend to eschew the three- and four-room B&B's that seem to have proliferated in recent years, not just in the Southwest but throughout the nation. In our travels, we've unfortunately visited too many small inns where the hosts were overbearing or unseasoned, and where we felt like uncomfortable strangers in someone else's home.

We have no such misgivings about recommending Casa de las Chimeneas, the proverbial small package in which good things really do come. At this charming hideaway, you'll be welcomed by skilled innkeepers who won't smother you with their presence, and you'll immediately feel comfortable and cozy in your room. Each room, by the way, has its own private outdoor entry.

Hidden behind seven-foot-tall adobe walls in a well-tended neighborhood less than three blocks from Taos Plaza, the inn, our Taos favorite, is named for the many chimneys whose fireplaces warm the interior. The setting is lovely, with expansive gardens that burst with colorful flowers from spring through fall. Cottonwood trees sway gently above an outdoor hot tub on the inn's back patio.

ROOMS FOR ROMANCE

A six-foot-long jetted tub-and-shower combination awaits in the privately situated Territorial Room (mid $200 range). Other features of this ultra-romantic accommodation include a motorized skylight, a gas-log fireplace, a viga ceiling, and heated *saltillo*-tiled floor.

Also designed with romantics in mind, La Sala de Patron (low $300 range) has both a spa tub for two and a shower designed for the two of you. The king-sized bed with its floor-to-ceiling carved posts faces a fireplace. A separate sitting room holds a love seat. This room shares a patio with the Sombraje Room.

Offered in the low $300 range, the newly remodeled five-hundred-square-foot Library Suite includes a private walled patio, a homey sitting room with a beamed ceiling, a wood floor, built-in bookshelves, a sofa sleeper, a kiva fireplace, and a game table. One step down is the bedroom, in which a king-sized bed sits on a brick floor. There's another kiva fireplace here, and the luxurious bathroom boasts a spa tub for two and a separate romantic steam shower with a waterfall feature.

Garden (low to mid $200 range), has pine floors, a kiva fireplace, a sitting area, and a king-sized bed with a hand-carved headboard. A skylight illuminates the shower and deep soaking tub for one.

THE FACTS

Nine rooms, each with private bath and private entry; five with fireplaces. Complimentary full breakfast served at tables for two and four or in your room. Communal hot tub. No disabled access. Pets welcome in certain rooms. Two-night minimum stay required during some weekends, three-night minimum during holiday periods. Moderate.

GETTING THERE

From northbound Highway 68 in downtown Taos, turn east on Kit Carson Road and follow to Witt Road. Turn right and follow to inn on right.

**OLD TAOS GUESTHOUSE
BED AND BREAKFAST**
1028 Witt Road
Taos, NM 87571
Telephone: (505) 758-5448;
toll-free: (800) 758-5448
www.oldtaos.com

OLD TAOS GUESTHOUSE BED AND BREAKFAST

Visit the historic Kit Carson home in Taos, and you'll get a taste of what life might have been like here in the mid-1800s. It was during this period in Taos's romantic history that a trapper built a little adobe at the base of the mountains, just up the road from the home of Kit and his new bride, Josefa.

In the late 1980s, the little hacienda, which had been expanded from time to time over the years, was renovated by ski enthusiasts Tim and Leslie Reeves, who transformed it into an exceptional inn. The long-time innkeepers have achieved and maintained a perfect balance between historic authenticity and contemporary romantic comforts.

Located just under two miles from the Taos Plaza in the Cañon neighborhood, the seven-acre property offers sweeping views of Taos Valley. Three earth-colored wings face a small courtyard lawn, and Adirondack-style chairs sit outside guest room doors under beamed verandas.

ROOMS FOR ROMANCE

At Old Taos Guesthouse, we discovered two of the most romantic rooms in all of Taos: the Sunset Suite and the Taos Suite. The Sunset Suite (mid $100 range) is a spacious hideaway with a step-up sitting area where two Taos-style chairs face a gas kiva fireplace flanked by small *bancos*. The king-sized Taos-style bed sits under a ceiling with vigas and *latillas,* and the tiny pueblo-style bathroom has a shower stall.

Offered for just a few dollars more is the Taos Suite, which features hardwood floors, a full kitchen, a viga ceiling, a couch, and two easy chairs. A *banco* that juts from the enchanting woodburning kiva fireplace separates the bed area from the sitting room. The king-sized bed is placed on a two-step platform under a large window overlooking trees and lawn. A cozy bathroom with wall murals holds a clawfoot tub.

Room 7 (under $100) faces the backyard and boasts an eighty-mile vista of Taos Valley as well as a view of wonderful sunsets. This 180-year-old room has hardwood floors, a viga ceiling, and thick adobe walls. The bathroom has a shower and a hand-painted tile sink, one of several pieces designed by innkeeper Tim.

Room 5 (under $100) is a private corner room in which a queen-sized bed is placed under an octagonal window and a painted beam ceiling. The bathroom has a large tiled shower.

THE FACTS

Six rooms, each with private bath. Complimentary full breakfast served at a communal table. No disabled access. Two-night minimum stay required during weekends; three-night minimum during holiday periods. Moderate.

GETTING THERE

From Highway 68, called Paseo del Pueblo Sur in Taos, turn west into plaza and drive straight onto Don Fernando. Drive two blocks, turn left on Manzanares, and turn right on Juanita Lane. Follow to inn on right.

LA POSADA DE TAOS
309 Juanita Lane
Taos, NM 87571
Telephone: (505) 758-8164;
toll-free: (800) 645-4803
www.laposadadetaos.com

Taos may be one of the Southwest's most popular destinations, but don't assume that a weekend here will necessarily drain your bank account. At this historic adobe, located in a quiet neighborhood just two blocks from Taos Plaza, we discovered some of the region's most moderately priced romantic rooms. In fact, La Posada de Taos just might be the Southwest's best romantic value.

Reportedly the first B&B in Taos, the inn has passed through various owners and was for sale at the time of our last visit.

ROOMS FOR ROMANCE

Offered at the time of our visit for around $200, La Casa de la Luna de Miel (the Honeymoon House) is a bargain-priced hideaway for romantics. This freestanding love nest is situated within the walls of the property but is about thirty feet from the inn's front door—plenty of space to ensure privacy. Inside, a seperate bedroom holds a king-sized bed and a gas stove. There's also a sitting area with a kiva fireplace and a private, walled courtyard. The bathroom has a spa tub for two.

Another romantic option is El Solecito (mid $100 range), a split-level room with brick-and-tile floors. A king-sized bed sits on the slightly raised upper level, adjacent to a sitting room with two willow chairs and a large kiva fireplace. Antique Mexican doors open onto a private patio, and the two-level tiled bathroom has a spa tub under a skylight.

Beutler (mid $100 range), the largest room in the house, has a private entrance, a king-sized bed, a couch, two Mexican-style chairs, and a kiva fireplace. The nice bathroom contains a Southwestern-style adobe shower stall and a spa tub into which the two of you might be able to squeeze.

The Liño Room (mid $100 range) holds a raised kiva fireplace and a queen-sized bed with a headboard resembling a picket fence. There's also a private patio. The tiny bathroom contains a shower stall and an antique washstand.

INN ON LA LOMA PLAZA

315 Ranchitos Road
P.O. Box 4159
Taos, NM 87571
Telephone: (505) 758-1717;
toll-free: (800) 530-3040
www.vacationtaos.com

THE FACTS

Seven rooms, each with private bath, fireplace, CD player, and videocassette player. Complimentary full breakfast served at tables for two and four. Complimentary afternoon and early-evening refreshments. Communal spa. Pool, tennis, and health club privileges. No disabled access. Two-night minimum stay required during weekends; three- to six-night minimum stay during holiday periods. Moderate to deluxe.

GETTING THERE

From northbound Highway 68 in Taos, turn left at first stoplight onto Paseo del Cañón and drive two blocks to first stop sign. Turn right on Salazar. Follow for approximately two miles to first stoplight and turn left on Ranchitos Road. Inn is on right.

INN ON LA LOMA PLAZA

You could spend a week in Taos without stumbling on this delightful upscale inn set on a gentle tree-shaded hill a scant three blocks from the plaza. Hidden behind two-hundred-year-old walls with minimal signage, the inn overlooks Taos and the Sangre de Cristo Range, as well as Taos Mountain.

Formerly known as Taos Hacienda Inn, this property is generally regarded as one of the community's poshest bed-and-breakfast inns. With its graceful balconies, covered and beamed porches, patios, and warming kivas, this resplendent pueblo-style structure oozes Southwestern romance. The public rooms are warm and inviting, and the guest quarters feature updated appointments and fresh flowers. Thick interior walls add charm as well as privacy.

Husband-and-wife innkeepers Jerry and Peggy Davis, the creators of this romantic haven, divide their time between Taos and Colorado, where both were active in civic affairs. Peggy is a former mayor of Vail and Jerry held the mayor's post in Avon.

ROOMS FOR ROMANCE

The inn's most decadent accommodation is Carey's Studio (low $300 range), a second-floor guest house suite that's tucked behind a Dutch-style door under the branches of an old elm tree. Windows on three walls provide nice vistas, including Taos Mountain.

Named for local artist Carey Moore, who once painted here, the suite is spacious and luxurious, featuring a fireplace, a couch, and a bed placed *banco*-style against a wall of windows. The studio features a king-sized bed, a kitchenette, and a private outdoor sitting area. The bathroom has a tiled tub-and-shower combination.

La Loma (mid to upper $200 range) has a private outdoor entrance, a kitchenette, and a pine-floored sitting room equipped with a couch, a kiva fireplace, and a table and chairs. The step-up bed landing with a viga ceiling holds a king-sized bed with a headboard embellished with decorative tin. The suite also has a tiny private patio.

A rocking horse and Old West knickknacks adorn Happy Trails (low to mid $200 range), which has knotty pine paneling, windows on three sides, a fireplace with a tiled hearth, and a queen-sized brass bed. French doors provide access to a private outdoor sitting area. The contemporary but tiny bathroom is outfitted with a tiled tub-and-shower combination.

For the economy minded, Wildrose (mid $100 range) is a cozy hideaway on the second floor, with a raised kiva fireplace, sponge-painted walls, *latilla* shutters, and a *latilla*-style headboard on the queen-sized bed. This value-priced room has a plaza view and a step-up tiled bathroom containing a tub-and-shower combination.

99

THE FACTS

Eleven rooms, each with private bath and CD player; eight with fireplaces. Complimentary full breakfast. Hot tub. Health club privileges. Limited disabled access. Two-night minimum stay required during weekends; three-night minimum during holiday periods. Moderate to deluxe.

GETTING THERE

From downtown Taos, follow Highway 68 north, which veers left and becomes Highway 64. One mile north of Taos Inn, watch for inn's sign and a gravel road on right. Follow gravel road past large rocks to inn on left.

HACIENDA DEL SOL
Highway 64
Taos, NM 87571
Telephone: (505) 758-0287;
toll-free: (866) 333-4459
www.taoshaciendadelsol.com

On a warm summer night, listen closely and you may hear drums from nearby Taos Pueblo. Soak in the outdoor hot tub and you might be treated to a dance of lightning over distant Taos Mountain. At Hacienda del Sol, the pueblo dwellers are your neighbors and Taos Mountain, as the innkeepers say, "is our backyard."

One of Taos' most historic properties, the inn was once part of the estate of the late Mabel Dodge Luhan, a well-known Taos art patroness whose houseguests included Georgia O'Keeffe and D. H. Lawrence.

The rambling tree-shaded estate, set back a comfortable distance off Highway 64 and abutting open Indian lands, consists of three adobe buildings, the oldest of which was constructed in the early 1800s. Traditional touches here include viga ceilings with *latillas,* arched doorways, and thick adobe walls. Pretty quilts adorn every bed.

ROOMS FOR ROMANCE

Our favorite is Los Amantes (low $300 range), a captivating suite in the main house, featuring a private patio entry via French doors. A picture window overlooks a shaded lawn area, and the beautiful ceiling features pine vigas and aspen *latillas.* A huge spa tub for two sits in a mahogany frame in a separate room under a viga ceiling and a skylight. The bathroom contains a combination steam- and drenching rain-forest-style shower.

The Taos Suite (high $100 range), is equipped with a queen-sized bed, two rocking chairs facing a gas fireplace, and a large bathroom with a skylit spa tub for two.

Furnished with a king-sized bed, Southwestern collectibles, an overstuffed chair, and a Taos-style drum table, the Adobe Room (upper $100 range) is another romantic choice. This charmer also has an ornate kiva fireplace with *nichos* and a viga-and-*latilla* ceiling. You'll step up to a sunny bathroom with double sinks and a shower that also functions as a steam room.

The Cowgirl Room (mid $200 range) boasts an impressive view of Taos Mountain through a large picture window. The second-floor room also features a gas fireplace and a pair of chairs, and the luxurious bathroom has a spa tub for two and a Mexican-tiled shower and steam room.

**CASA EUROPA BED-AND-BREAKFAST
INN AND GALLERY**

840 Upper Ranchitos Road
P.O. Box 3F
Taos, NM 87571
Telephone: (505) 758-9798;
toll-free: (888) 758-9798
www.casaeuropanm.com

THE FACTS

*Seven rooms, each with private bath, fireplace, and sitting
area. Complimentary full breakfast served at communal
table. Complimentary afternoon refreshments. Hot tub
and sauna. No disabled access. Two-night minimum stay
required during weekends; three- to five-night minimum
during holiday periods. Moderate.*

GETTING THERE

*From Highway 68 in Ranchos de Taos, turn west on
Highway 240/Lower Ranchitos Road and follow past
Martinez Hacienda. Turn left on Upper Ranchitos Road
and follow to inn on left.*

CASA EUROPA BED-AND-BREAKFAST
INN AND GALLERY

On the lookout for what had been described as a two-century-old adobe, we passed right by Casa Europa the first time, mistaking the inn's contemporary-style, multiwindowed façade for that of a newer private home.

The expanse of glass not only creates a warm and romantic ambience, it showcases an appealing and restful country setting that sets Casa Europa apart from most of our other Taos destinations. It's refreshingly quiet and peaceful out here, yet the town plaza is only a two-minute drive away. The room rates are also quite reasonable.

ROOMS FOR ROMANCE

Situated off the center courtyard and accessed through a sliding door, the Spa Suite (high $100 range) is a house favorite. A king-sized bed sits on a heated *saltillo*-tiled floor near a fireplace. Adjacent to a comfortable sitting area with a leather couch and a television is a raised and tiled spa tub for two. The bathroom contains a shower that doubles as a steam sauna.

The Apartment Suite (high $100 range) was at one time a private residence. As such, it's fully equipped with a kitchen and a dining area; a living room with a sofa, a corner kiva fireplace, and *banco* seating; a bedroom with a king-sized bed; a marble bathroom; and a spa tub for two in a seperate room.

In the French Room (mid $100 range), a striking century-old queen-sized brass bed from France is centered on a hand-hewn wood floor that's also over a hundred years old. Above is a beautiful white coved viga ceiling. A kiva fireplace is visible from the bed. The marble bathroom has a shower, and French doors open onto a courtyard.

The Southwest Suite (upper $100 range) is a large second-floor hideaway with views of the surrounding mountains. A king-sized bed sits in an alcove adjacent to a sitting room with a porcelain wood stove, a love seat, and a writing desk. The bathroom has a shower and a spa tub for one.

The corner Willow Room (mid $100 range) has a very cozy sitting room with a kiva fireplace and *banco* seating.

THE FACTS

Five rooms, each with private bath, fireplace, CD player, and tub for two. Complimentary full breakfast served at tables for two or more or delivered to your room. Complimentary afternoon and evening refreshments. Spa. Disabled access. No minimum night stay required. Moderate to expensive.

GETTING THERE

From Taos Plaza, follow Highway 64 north for four miles to Highway 150. Turn right and follow Highway 150 for about two and a half miles. Bear left onto State Highway 230 and follow for just under two miles to County Road B-143. Turn left and follow a half mile to inn's sign on left.

**ALMA DEL MONTE—
SPIRIT OF THE MOUNTAIN B&B**
372 Hondo Seco Road
P.O. Box 617
Taos, NM 87571
Telephone: (505) 776-2721;
toll-free: (800) 273-7203
www.almaspirit.com

ALMA DEL MONTE—SPIRIT OF THE MOUNTAIN B&B

While most Taos-bound travelers set their sights on the historic plaza area, romantics in-the-know head north a few extra miles for the wide open spaces that surround Alma del Monte, our newest Taos discovery.

Built in recent years as a luxury inn, Alma del Monte is conveniently located along the route to Taos Ski Valley. However, skiers may end up trading a day on the slopes for a day spent more leisurely here by the fire, in a hammock, or in the courtyard spa.

The grand hacienda-style inn is positioned so as to take full advantage of spiritually mesmerizing vistas over the high-plains sagebrush to the Sangre de Cristo range. Actress Julia Roberts lives nearby. All rooms feature king-sized beds, *latilla* and viga ceilings, kiva fireplaces, and bathrooms with separate showers and spa tubs into which two friendly people might be able to squeeze.

ROOMS FOR ROMANCE

There's an antique fainting couch to catch you in the event the view—or your partner—takes your breath away in the Taos Room (mid $200 range). This honeymoon favorite has a hand-painted king-sized four-poster bed, a kiva fireplace, and access to a private garden.

A beautiful iron-framed bed with a delicate hand-knotted canopy makes the Wheeler Room (high $100 range) another romantic favorite. Guests here also enjoy a small private garden and a gas kiva fireplace sitting area with a pair of chairs.

If the two of you are inspired by sunsets, Pedernal (high $100 range) is your best bet. It faces the southwest and offers grand views of mountains and mesas as well as the lights of Taos. This room is equipped with a king-sized leather-upholstered bed and two chairs.

The spacious Sangre de Cristo Room (mid $200 range) has as its centerpiece a handsome bed whose carved mahogany headboard stands over seven feet in height. Even the bathroom in this nice end room boasts an inspiring view.

THE FACTS

Seven rooms and suites, each with private bath; four with woodburning fireplaces. Solarium with lap pool, spa, sauna, and fitness room. No disabled access. Two-night minimum stay required during weekends; four-night minimum during holiday periods. Moderate to expensive.

GETTING THERE

From downtown Taos, follow Highway 68/Paseo del Pueblo Norte north out of town. It becomes Highway 522 north of Taos. Five miles north of Taos Plaza, turn right on Highway 150/Taos Ski Valley Road and follow to Taos Ski Valley. At resort, follow road as it loops around large parking area and turns right onto Thining Road. Turn right on Pattison Loop Road and follow to inn.

CHALET MONTESANO

Unlike many charmless resort area accommodations we've visited, which seem to exist solely for the purpose of providing a few hours of sleep for skiers, Chalet Montesano is a breath of fresh mountain air.

Hidden away among the pines above the busy Taos Ski Valley village center, this former private residence is within easy walking distance of the lifts. In the warmer months, visitors will find the inn a convenient base for day hikes and mountain bike excursions.

Skiers are provided with conveniences such as ski packages, a ski boot dryer, and a clothes washer and dryer. Nonskiers can work out in a well-equipped exercise room or in the indoor lap pool. There's also a spa for those après-ski evenings and summer nights.

ROOMS FOR ROMANCE

For a romantic getaway, we definitely recommend the two Alpine studio apartments on the third floor. These six-hundred-square-foot units have kitchens, fireplaces, dining and living areas, queen-sized Murphy beds, and bathrooms with tub-and-shower combinations. The two third-floor studios share a mountain-view deck. There's another Alpine studio on the ground floor that lacks a balcony.

Even more spacious is the inn's one-bedroom apartment (high $200 range), with a living room boasting a three-sided fireplace, a bedroom with a king-sized bed, a kitchen, a view balcony, and a sleeping loft.

We also liked the rooms in the "Standard" category that have views. These carry rates in the high $100 range. A couple of rooms located on the inn's ground floor are not as bright and cheery as those on the higher levels.

All rooms are equipped with a television, telephone, and audio system. The rates noted above are for winter. Summer tariffs are considerably less.

CHALET MONTESANO
1 Pattison Loop Road
P.O. Box 77
Taos Ski Valley, NM 87525
Telephone: (505) 776-8226;
toll-free: (800) 723-9104
www.chaletmontesano.com

DAYTIME DIVERSIONS

The magnificent cliff dwellings of the Anasazi Indians
are preserved at Mesa Verde National Park, southeast of
CORTEZ. One of the structures, Cliff Palace, is the largest
of its kind in the world.

The Durango Silverton Narrow Gauge Railroad operates very popular forty-five-mile excursions through the
mountains between charming DURANGO and the historic
burg of SILVERTON.

Adventurous visitors can raft the Animas River or rent
a four-wheel-drive vehicle and visit remote ALTA, a mountain
ghost town located about thirty minutes outside Durango.

The Purgatory-Durango ski resort, twenty-five miles
north of DURANGO, is also a popular summertime destination, offering alpine slide rides, mountain biking trails,
and music concerts.

The route along Highways 145 and 160 from MANCOS
and CORTEZ to TELLURIDE is part of the scenic San Juan
Skyway, affording vistas ranging from red-rock formations to
fourteen-thousand-foot-high snow peaks.

TABLES FOR TWO

- Dolores River Brewery, 100 South Fourth Street, DOLORES
- Kennebec Café and Bakery, 4 County Road 124, HESPERUS
- Ken and Sue's Place, 636 Main Avenue, DURANGO
- Beau Jo's Mountain Bistro, 400 South Camino Del Rio,
  DURANGO
- Hamilton's Chop House, 39000 Highway 550 North,
  DURANGO

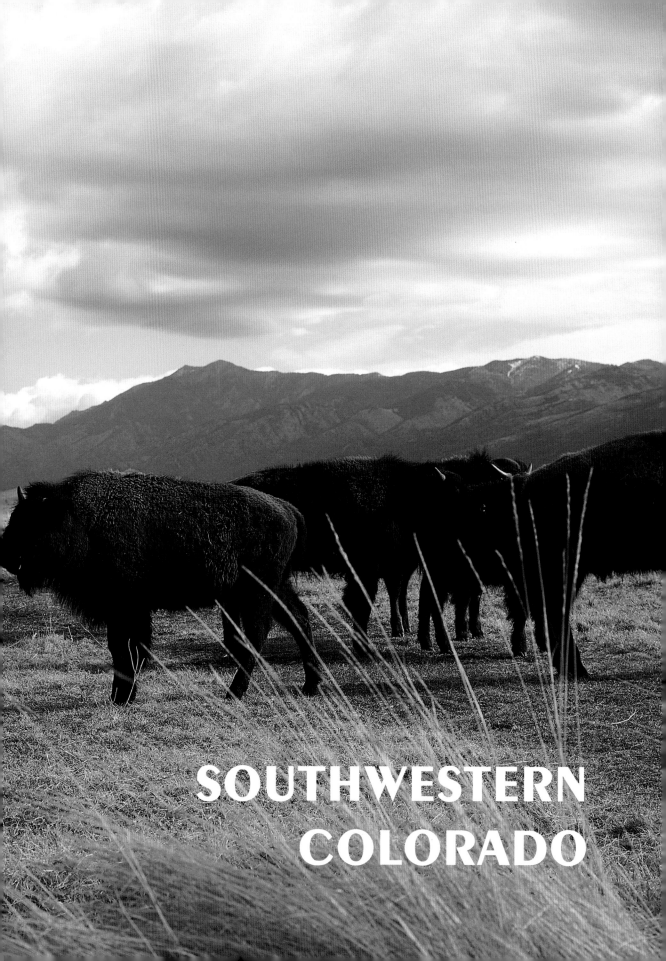

SOUTHWESTERN
COLORADO

THE FACTS

Eight rooms, each with private bath. Complimentary full breakfast served at communal table. Complimentary afternoon snacks. Limited disabled access. Two-night minimum stay required during weekends and holiday periods; three-night minimum during Christmas holidays. Moderate.

GETTING THERE

From Highway 160 in Durango, drive north through town on Highway 550 for approximately twelve miles to lodging sign on right. Turn right past mailboxes, then take an immediate right into inn's driveway. If you pass the KOA campground on Highway 550, you've gone too far north.

LOGWOOD

35060 Highway 550 North
Durango, CO 81301
Telephone: (970) 259-4396;
toll-free: (800) 369-4082
www.durango-logwoodinn.com

LOGWOOD

On our first visit, entering Durango from the south, we frankly wondered whether the community would prove to be a suitably romantic destination. The hills were sunburned and barren, and charmless buildings lined the highway.

Our impression improved as we drove through the busy, well-preserved downtown, and by the time we reached the green and woodsy northern outskirts we were completely smitten.

Logwood, an enchanting two-story log-walled structure about twelve miles north of Durango, takes full advantage of the beautiful Animas River valley. The inn is surrounded by trees and cuddles right up to the river. A large deck overlooks the hillside and the rushing water. Deer and beaver can often be seen from the inn's large deck. There's also a recreation room with a pool table, a piano, and a game table.

ROOMS FOR ROMANCE

At the time of our visit, rooms were being offered for as little as $100 per night during the high-season summer months. Winter rates were even less expensive, making Logwood an all-season romantic bargain.

The guest rooms and bathrooms are comparatively small, but each is equipped with the essentials. They all have large windows to take advantage of the glorious outdoors, and the log-frame beds are covered with colorful hand-stitched quilts.

One of the nicest rooms is Mesa Verde (low $100 range), a second-floor hideaway with a king-sized bed and a river-and-mountain view. The bathroom has a tub-and-shower combination.

Another romantic option is the Narrow Gauge Room (around $100), a main-level room offering a king-sized bed and a large bathroom with a five-foot-long soaking tub and a separate shower. The Cliff Palace Room (around $100) is also equipped with an oversized soaking tub for two.

In the Animas Suite (mid $100 range) on the lower level, French doors connect the two bedrooms, one with a queen-sized bed, the other with a king. There's a gas stove on the king side, and a private entry leads outside to the river. This is the perfect retreat for a couple with a child or two in tow.

THE FACTS

Ten rooms, each with private bath. Complimentary full breakfast served at communal table or tables for two. Complimentary afternoon refreshments. Disabled access. Two-night minimum stay preferred during holiday periods. Moderate to expensive.

GETTING THERE

From Durango, drive west on Highway 160 for three miles and turn right on Lightner Creek Road. Follow for one mile to inn on left.

LIGHTNER CREEK INN BED AND BREAKFAST

One of our most enjoyable tasks is touring the city streets, neighborhoods, and back roads of various communities and narrowing down long lists of local inns to find the most romantic. We discovered the standard-bearer of Durango in lovely Lightner Creek Canyon about four miles from town.

The canyon's namesake inn occupies a pastoral six-acre parcel that includes a pond, a delightful section of Lightner Creek, gardens, and a stand of tall cottonwoods. Bald eagles, wild turkeys, peregrine falcons, and mule deer are among the inhabitants of an adjacent wildlife refuge.

The inn itself began as an attractive turn-of-the-century cottage and has been enlarged and remodeled with obvious great care over the years. The furnishings are of high quality, and the public and guest rooms are tastefully decorated and nicely windowed.

ROOMS FOR ROMANCE

Our favorite room, the Alpine Retreat (low $200 range), is on the second level of the carriage house, which is located a few steps from the main inn. The seven-hundred-square-foot suite affords a view of aspen trees, the creek, and the nearby mountainside. The décor conjures images of a European ski lodge and is furnished with a fluffy king-sized bed, a queen-sized bed, a pair of wing chairs, and a pellet stove. French doors open onto a small deck. The spacious bathroom holds a large tiled shower that's big enough for the two of you.

Other romantic hideaways include the Wild Rose and Captain's Quarters (high $100 range), each with a spa tub, a king-sized bed, and a private patio. Captain's Quarters also has a kitchen.

The French Bouquet Room (low $100 range), a second-floor rear corner room, features an impressive queen-sized, high-backed bed, a wicker chaise, and a writing desk. This room brings in the Colorado sky with its two blue walls and complementary artwork. The large window provides a view of the pond, the gazebo, the creek, and the wooded hillside.

LIGHTNER CREEK INN BED AND BREAKFAST
999 County Road 207
Durango, CO 81301
Telephone: (970) 259-1226;
toll-free: (800) 268-9804
www.lightnercreekinn.com

BLUE LAKE RANCH

16919 Highway 140
Hesperus, CO 81326
Telephone toll-free: (888) 258-3525
www.bluelakeranch.com

THE FACTS

Sixteen rooms and cottages, each with private bath. Complimentary European-style breakfast buffet served in dining room at tables for two or more. Limited disabled access. Two-night minimum stay required during weekends; three-night minimum stay during holiday periods. Moderate to deluxe.

GETTING THERE

From Durango, follow Highway 160 west for eleven miles to Hesperus. Turn south on Highway 140 and drive for six and a half miles (use your odometer) to a gravel drive on the right. (Drive is a little over one mile north of Highway 141 junction.) Follow gravel drive to inn.

BLUE LAKE RANCH

To describe Blue Lake Ranch as an inn would be both a disservice and an understatement. It's more like a small romantic community, a utopia for lovers in which the population rarely exceeds twenty. Easily one of the most romantic destinations in the western states, the ranch provides an array of intimate environments that should satisfy the most discriminating couples.

A collection of cozy, first-rate bed-and-breakfast-style rooms and remote cottages, Blue Lake Ranch enjoys a very private mountain locale settled originally by a Swedish immigrant family. Innkeeper David Alford bought a large swath of land here in the late 1970s and set about renovating buildings and creating a comfortable retreat. During the renovation, he married, literally, the girl next door. Shirley, a physician, shares innkeeping duties. The couple also owns the Don Gaspar Inn in Santa Fe (see separate listing) and a newer property, Casa Blanca, in Farmington, New Mexico.

ROOMS FOR ROMANCE

Since our first visit, the ranch has grown to 240 acres and sixteen accommodations. One of our personal favorites is the Cabin on the Lake (low $300 range), a three-bedroom, three-bath cottage set on the shore of private Blue Lake, in which guests have been known to dip sans swimsuits. Crafted from logs and stone, the cabin has a wraparound deck with rocking chairs. The romantic loft bedroom contains a stone fireplace and a king-sized bed and boasts mountain views to die for. Downstairs is a rock fireplace and comfy Taos furniture.

Cottage in the Woods (around $200) is reached via a wooded path from the main inn. Set amid piñon trees and a private garden, the cottage has a kitchenette with *saltillo* tile, and a bathroom with an oval spa tub for two. The step-up bedroom, with a king-sized bed, has cedar paneling and an open-beam ceiling.

A little yellow homesteaders' cabin, now called River House (high $100), is nestled on the banks of La Plata River in a cottonwood grove about one mile from the ranch. The living room is appointed with wicker furniture and features a gas fireplace and television. There's also a *saltillo*-tiled kitchen. The bathroom holds a tub-and-shower combination, and one of the two bedrooms has a queen-sized bed.

Among the most popular accommodations for visiting romantics are the Oak Grove and Cedar Casitas, both offered in the low $200 range. The Oak Grove is decorated with Navajo rugs and baskets and has two indulgent bathrooms, one with a spa tub for two and another with a shower. The living room has a gas fireplace.

We also recommend the spacious and private Garden Room (high $100 range), with its Japanese-style walk-in shower and a deep soaking tub, and the Lake View Suite (high $100 range), which overlooks Blue Lake and has a gas fireplace and a spa tub for two.

THE FACTS

Five rooms, each with private bath. Complimentary full breakfast served at a communal table. Complimentary evening refreshments. Communal spa. Billiard room. No disabled access. Two-night minimum stay required during weekends and holiday periods. Moderate.

GETTING THERE

From Highway 160 in Mancos, follow Highway 184 northwest for ten miles to inn sign on right. Inn is about forty miles from Durango and about twenty miles from Mesa Verde cliff dwellings.

LOST CANYON LAKE LODGE

One of the northernmost of our fifty destinations, Lost Canyon Lake Lodge perches on a hill overlooking a pretty lake in the pines at a lofty elevation of over seven thousand feet. The lodge is located between the communities of Dolores and Mancos, and a number of attractions, including Durango's famous narrow-gauge railroad and Mesa Verde National Park, are within a short drive.

Operated by Tom and Sally Garrison, the two-story log structure has a covered wraparound porch and a scenic view deck facing a seemingly endless pine forest. Guests are invited to explore over twenty lush acres.

Also available to inn guests are a communal deck-mounted spa with a lake view, a hillside rock fire pit for cool mountain evenings, and a billiard table.

ROOMS FOR ROMANCE

For a romantic getaway, we recommend the inn's two king-bedded rooms and a cozy, fully equipped log cabin. The two rooms with king-sized beds (low $100 range) have vaulted ceilings, and soaring windows that overlook the lake and forest. They also have small sitting areas with chairs.

New since our first visit, the five-hundred-square-foot log cabin is perfect for traveling romantics. It's also a good choice for couples traveling with a child or two. The cabin has a living area with a love seat and a pair of chairs, a small kitchen, a bedroom with a queen-sized bed, and a sleeping loft that sleeps two on futons. The porch faces the lake and provides a private, quiet place for reading and relaxing.

LOST CANYON LAKE LODGE
15472 CR 35.3
Mancos, CO 81328
Telephone: (970) 882-7871
www.lostcanyonlakelodge.com

Glossary

If you're a first-time visitor to the Southwest, you'll likely hear or read a few unfamiliar words or see an unusual object or two. Following is a short glossary of terms that are common in this romantic region.

BANCO: A pueblo-style seat, typically of plaster, built into a wall, often near a kiva. These often-cushioned places to snuggle were built with romantics in mind. This type of seating is referred to as a daybed or a banquette elsewhere.

BULTOS: Wooden carvings of saints.

EQUIPALES: Mexican-style chairs and sofas whose seats and backs are constructed of stretched hide.

FAROLITO: A small bonfire. In the Santa Fe area it refers to a paper bag with sand in the bottom in which a lighted candle is placed (called a *luminaria* elsewhere).

KIVA: A beehive-shaped fireplace found in the corners of many Southwestern guest rooms.

KOKOPELLI: The Native American trickster and flute player whose visage graces many Southwestern objets d'art.

LATILLAS: Tightly spaced, rough-cut branches or strips of wood arranged as part of Southwestern-style doors and shutter frames or between ceiling *vigas.*

LUMINARIA: A paper bag with sand in the bottom in which a lighted candle is placed; called a *farolito* in the Santa Fe area.

NICHOS: Small recessed shelves in a wall or in a kiva fireplace where pottery and collectibles are displayed.

RETABLOS: Paintings on wood of religious figures.

RISTRA: A hanging decorative cluster of dried chilies.

SAGUARO: This stately cactus with arms is pronounced saw-WAH-row.

SALTILLO TILES: Mexican clay tiles.

TAOS-STYLE FURNITURE: Oversized, thick- and wide-cushioned chairs, sofas, and beds, often of log-frame construction. Some Taos sofas are large enough to also function as twin-sized beds.

VIGAS: Exposed log beams, often interspersed with plaster coving or *latillas,* which support the ceilings in many of the guest rooms described in this book.

VORTEX: In the Southwest, vortex describes places of spiritual energy. The Sedona and Santa Fe regions, for example, are believed to have numerous vortices.

Index

MORE RESOURCES FOR ROMANTIC TRAVELS

WEEKENDS FOR TWO IN NORTHERN CALIFORNIA: 50 ROMANTIC GETAWAYS

The original romantic travel guide that started it all, now in its fourth edition.

WEEKENDS FOR TWO IN THE WINE COUNTRY: 50 ROMANTIC NORTHERN CALIFORNIA GETAWAYS

Destinations from Mendocino County to the wine country of the Central Coast.

WEEKENDS FOR TWO IN SOUTHERN CALIFORNIA: 50 ROMANTIC GETAWAYS

Intimate destinations from the Santa Barbara coast to the sultry desert, now in its third edition.

WEEKENDS FOR TWO IN THE PACIFIC NORTHWEST: 50 ROMANTIC GETAWAYS

Coastal, mountain, and island hideaways in Oregon, Washington, and western British Columbia.

WEEKENDS FOR TWO IN NEW ENGLAND: 50 ROMANTIC GETAWAYS

Places of the heart in Maine, Vermont, New Hampshire, Massachusetts, Connecticut, and Rhode Island.

With more than 150 color photographs and hundreds of room descriptions in each book, these are the definitive travel guides to the nation's most romantic destinations. All are authored by Bill Gleeson and published by Chronicle Books. For additional information about these volumes, please visit www.billgleeson.com. Your opinions are critical.

CAST YOUR VOTE!

THE SOUTHWEST'S MOST ROMANTIC HOTEL OR INN

Complete and mail this form to Bill Gleeson, *Weekends for Two,* Chronicle Books, 85 Second Street, Sixth Floor, San Francisco, CA 94105.

Our favorite Southwest romantic retreat (does not have to be featured in this book):

NAME OF HOTEL/INN: _____

CITY/TOWN: _____

THIS PLACE IS SPECIAL BECAUSE: _____

_____

_____

_____

_____

_____